D1544955

SARTRE
ROMANTIC RATIONALIST

SARTRE

ROMANTIC RATIONALIST

Iris Murdoch

VIKING

VIKING
Viking Penguin Inc.
40 West 23rd Street,
New York, New York 10010, U.S.A.

First American Edition
Published in 1987

ISBN 0–670–81726–0

Library of Congress Catalog Card Number 86–40566
(CIP data available)

Printed in Great Britain by
Redwood Burn Limited, Trowbridge, Wiltshire

CONTENTS

INTRODUCTION

Philosophers are not often popular idols, and works of philosophy rarely become guide-books to living, during the philosopher's lifetime. In the twenty years after the war Sartre was probably the best-known metaphysician in Europe, best-known that is not just among professional thinkers (many of whom ignored him) but among young and youngish people who, for once, found in philosophy, in his philosophy, the clear and inspiring explanation of the world which philosophers are generally supposed to provide. The fundamental and attractive idea was freedom. It had long been known that God was dead and that man was self-created. Sartre produced a fresh and apt picture of this self-chosen being. The metaphysical imagery of *L'Être et le Néant, Being and Nothingness*, was, for popular purposes, easily grasped. The *pour-soi*, for-itself, a spontaneous free consciousness, was contrasted with the *en-soi*, in itself, inert, fixed, unfree. The *en-soi* was the world experienced as alien, senselessly contingent or unreflectively deformed. The heroic consciousness, the individual self, inalienably and ineluctably free, challengingly confronted the 'given', in the form of existing society, history, tradition, other people. The war was over, Europe was in ruins, we had emerged from a long captivity, all was to be remade. Sartre's philosophy was an inspiration to many who felt that they must, and *could*, make out of all that misery and chaos a better world, for it had now been revealed that any-

9

thing was possible. Existentialism was the new religion, the new salvation. This was the atmosphere in
Brussels in 1945 where I first read *L'Être et le Néant* and
where I briefly (and on this occasion only) met Sartre.
His presence in the city was like that of a pop star.
Chico Marx, who was there at about the same time,
was less rapturously received. The only other occasion
when I saw a philosopher being hailed as a prophet
was in California in 1984 when I attended a lecture by
Jacques Derrida (*Un autre temps, toujours la même France*).

One of the charms of the Sartrian philosophy at that
moment was that it readily carried a political message.
The enemy was the past, the old bourgeois world with
its clumsy mechanism and its illusions and its fatal
mistakes. It was and must be the end of an era.
Fascism had been destroyed, left-wing governments
would come to power everywhere, and in England one
promptly did. It is interesting, and indeed touching,
that so much optimism arose out of the vaguest understanding of Sartre's doctrine, which also carried the
melancholy message that since the *pour-soi* can never
be united with the *en-soi*, man is *une passion inutile*, a
useless, futile, passion. The darker message of the doctrine was unnoticed, or became itself a source of
energy, perhaps because, as in the case of other so-
called pessimists such as Hume or Schopenhauer, the
cordial and self-satisfied discourse of the thinker
conveys a cheering vitality quite at odds with his
theory. The *en-soi*, an alien object of fascination, of
fear, even of hate, in Sartre's obsessive and hypnotic
world picture, appears in his philosophical novel *La
Nausée* as contingent matter, our surroundings, things,
experienced as senseless and awful. In *L'Être et le Néant*
and also in the novel sequence *Les Chemins de la Liberté*,

the *en-soi* appears, in contrast to free reflection, as inert conventional opinions, dead traditions, illusions. In the drama *Huis Clos*, which was received with enthusiasm and is still played, the alien being is another person, whose freedom contradicts one's own, and whose unassimilable Medusa gaze turns one's *pour-soi* into an *en-soi*. This imagery returns us to the realisation that the 'hero' of Sartre's early philosophy is, like the Cartesian subject, alone.

In his elegant account of his childhood, *Les Mots*, Sartre, brought up, he tells us, by two women and an old man, was early aware of himself as an actor, uncertainly enacting his role as a child prodigy, unable to find and coincide with his real self. This, already, was expressive of the *inutile* metaphysical passion which fills and inspires his work, longing to devour the world and make it his own, together with a tormenting and invigorating consciousness of the impossibility of success. The model which seems to prove that such a *total* philosophical synthesis can be, very nearly, achieved is Hegel's *Phenomenology of Mind*, and it has been the dream of more than one metaphysically minded thinker, after and including Marx, to rewrite this book and get it right. Sartre attempted it twice. *L'Être et le Néant* was a huge non-historical revision of the subject-object dialectic, in which the prime value, and motive force, replacing Hegel's *Geist*, was freedom (individual project), and wherein the insights of Heidegger (whose mythology Sartre secularised), Husserl, Freud and Marx were all to be accommodated. Sartre here portrayed the dialectic psychologically as the human soul; later he portrayed it socio-politically as human history. His later work remains, for all its obvious divergence and new tone, significantly close, his critics would say too close, to the first fine careless rapture of the early synthesis.

Sartre is, in himself, as philosopher, novelist, playwright, literary critic, biographer, essayist, journalist, a remarkable instance of the universal omnivorous writer. *La Nausée*, Sartre's celebration of the horror of the contingent, is one of the very few unadulterated and successful members of the genre 'philosophical novel'. It is unique in Sartre's work, and I think in literature generally, a young man's *tour de force*. The unfinished sequence *Les Chemins de la Liberté* are by contrast traditional novels, crammed with characters, events, story, various people, various moral judgements. Sartre evidently had, at this stage, no difficulty in telling a story, a feat which later on writers (and perhaps he) felt to be more difficult and problematic. These novels have a huge subject, passionately grasped and felt, the outbreak of war and the occupation of France, and they retain their power as works of literature. There are fairly inconspicuous moments of philosophical reflection, but these are not in any formidable or purposive sense 'existentialist novels', and their hero, Mathieu, is not a didactically existentialist hero. Indeed he appears, in comparison with more extreme and bizarre pictures of the human person conjured up elsewhere in Sartre's philosophical and literary writings, and in spite of being periodically exhausted by the futile vagueness of his thoughts, a pillar of sobriety and decency, possessing quite ordinary qualities including a traditional moral sense. Short stories, in the collection *Le Mur*, explore a Sartrian existentialist idea, evident in Sartre's followers and indeed in late romantic literature generally, that authentic being is attained in extreme situations, and

in revolt against society. Here the figures who fascinate Sartre are often violent, even criminal. Hatred of
existing (Western) society, often identified as 'bourgeois society' and contrasted with some imagined
alternative, has of course been a long-standing (and
often fruitful) source of literary inspiration. Sartre
later indulged and explained his admiration for stylish
and talented criminals in his long book about Jean
Genet. He continued his literary career not as a story-
teller but as a, successful, writer of plays. The plays
were propaganda as well as art, and could be seen as
supplementary to the battling articles in *Temps
Modernes*. But perhaps in the long run the play satisfied
the literary Sartre because of its compulsory formal
brevity. The metaphysician who could not say anything unless he said everything was compelled in the
theatre to give his message briefly; and as Sartre unfor-
tunately could not *do* everything, as opposed to *thinking*
everything, he found the theatre, where he had un-
doubted talent, a sympathetic place to drop into.

It often remains a mystery, in spite of hard work
done on the subject by spectators including Sartre
himself, why artists suddenly stop doing something
they are good at and do nothing, or something else,
which of course they may be good at too. Sartre might
have gone on to write a huge novel full of thoughts and
people. He did not, instead he wrote a book about Baudelaire, a long book about Jean Genet, and an extremely long book about Flaubert. These works come,
strictly speaking, under the head of existential psychoanalysis, a procedure outlined in *L'Être et le Néant*, not
under that of literary criticism. *Les Mots*, presumably
an instance of existential self-analysis, is calm, even
cold in tone. The other books, more passionate, in

attempting to show in detail how the persons in question came to choose themselves to be as they were, also reveal Sartre's own identification with, and sense of similarity to, his chosen subjects, and his intent desire to re-create himself inside them. On the other hand he appears, especially in the book on Flaubert, *L'Idiot de la Famille*, as a meticulous historian. The role of historian is one which he more positively assumes in his later philosophical synthesis. Of the book on Genet, it may be said that it expresses not only Sartre's particular hatred of society, but his hatred of religion, one might say his religious hatred of religion. He says in *Les Mots* that atheism is a cruel long-term business. *L'Être et le Néant* was attacked by critics who found it not only Godless but immoral, recognising no value except a Luciferian private will which in effect exalted unprincipled 'sincerity', bizarre originality, and irresponsible courage. The conclusion of *Huis Clos*, and one message of *L'Être et le Néant*, is that *l'enfer c'est les autres*, hell is other people, all men are enemies, an expression of desperate or insolent solipsism which left no place for love or duty or the complex network of ordinary morals. Such metaphysical simplification also, by a shift to a political perspective, made room for the sinister message that in an oppressive society only violence is honest.

Sartre pursued his demonic 'other' in his studies of Baudelaire, Genet, and Flaubert: Baudelaire, *le poète maudit*, social rebel, feminine temperament, masochist, caught in his own master and slave dialectic of revolt and submission, Genet, foundling, criminal, artist, feminine homosexual, boldly taking his own will as his conscience while accepting the moral judgements of society, Flaubert, also poised between rebellion and obedience, atheism and faith, another feminine temperament who actually became a woman in the person of his famous heroine. Both Baudelaire and Flaubert have a bourgeois background from which they escape by a *déclassement symbolique*, by electing themselves, as artists, into an imaginary elite academy or spiritual nobility; Genet is without, at least these, illusions. *L'Être et le Néant* was published in 1943, the book on Baudelaire in 1946, the book on Genet in 1952, the *Critique de la Raison Dialectique*, Sartre's second synthesis, in 1960, *L'Idiot de la Famille*, three volumes on Flaubert, nearly 4000 pages, in 1971–72. The remarkable study of Genet, the 'diabolical saint', (*Saint Genet: Comédien et Martyr*) is an exercise in Sartre's own *déclassement*, his escape from 'bourgeois morality' and the benign Kantian perspectives of *Existentialism and Humanism*. It is thus a doorway into the later Marxist–Existentialist phase of his thought. He compares Genet with Bukharin, Genet is 'a bourgeois Bukharin'; Bukharin confesses his guilt, judging himself upon Marxist principles which, against himself, he humbly affirms, so committing 'moral suicide'. Genet also confesses, in accordance with the bourgeois values which brand him as wicked, as a murderer and a thief; but since, while doing so, he refuses to deny himself as a free self-willing subject whose will is his own rightness and justice, he is able to receive with proud satisfaction the judgement of society which makes of him an object, a criminal, a non-person, a prisoner without a future. Thus Genet (almost) achieves the impossible, of being object and subject, *être et néant*, all at once. In the course of the book Sartre manages to transform a (simplified) psychological analysis into a (simplified) political message. He examines the various dialectical 'ploys' of the Genet personality. Genet's relations with others take (for instance) the form of wanting to *be* the other, but since he can only achieve this as fantasy, the other that he wills to be turns out to be a mere appearance; he finds there only 'empty shells, dead bodies, abandoned houses', and is returned to his, equally absent, self, an object, a solitary, beneath a relentless light (*lux perpetua?*), unable to escape the judgement of others, but unable to encounter them either. Sartre finally offers us Genet as personifying the futility of the bourgeois subject who is condemned to maintain values which he (really) knows to be empty and vanishing. Genet is redeemed, is saint, martyr, edifying exemplar, and hero of our time, because he lives this condition with full awareness to both extremes, both as subject and object, accepting (like Saint Teresa as Sartre points out) all accusations against him as having some substance. But he is better than Saint Teresa because she is supported by 'general esteem' and he is not. (To put it, absurdly, in Kierkegaardian terms, Saint Teresa is a tragic hero while Genet is a true Knight of Faith.) Genet is worthy of our attention, Sartre argues, because he is sincerely and openly and extremely what we, bourgeois, are secretly, timidly and hypocritically. He suffers, while we evade suffering. Genet is also of course (and for some of us more obviously) redeemed by becoming an artist. He is, again like Baudelaire, a dandy, a feminine soul, he is 'metamorphosed into a lover, that is into a woman'. He becomes an aesthete, progresses to writing poetry, at last becomes a talented writer. Sartre said in the book on Baudelaire that he was not offering literary criticism. At the same time, most explicitly in the Flaubert book, he wishes to discover how just *this* man (so like many others in general respects) becomes *this* artist. But such a discovery, in so far as it can be made at all, should emerge from critical study of the artist's work. Sartre even when he does talk about the work, is more concerned with expounding it as a continuous and unitary manifestation of Genet's psychology. In order to present Genet (ultimately) as political propaganda, Sartre oversimplifies his picture of this extraordinary man, obscuring another Genet who has developed other virtues, to some extent shared by the bourgeois, those of the good artist, industry, patience, humility, truthfulness. To suggest that, partly through success, Genet may in later life have become, as we ordinarily say, 'a better man', would be alien to Sartre's purpose. At the end of the book, where Sartre attributes to his hero the virtue of generosity, he has to explain that this is simply an expression of freedom, and that in any case generosity is alienated by its context in bourgeois property relations. The original metaphysical distinction between *être et néant, mauvaise foi* and freedom, increasingly appears as the contrast between corrupt collapsing bourgeois society and some ideal, as yet unclarified, which under present conditions can only sincerely express itself as revolt. Indeed, if we are sincere, Sartre suggests, we have a choice between the humility of Bukharin, deliberate surrender of freedom and moral suicide, and the pride of Genet, who asserts the value of his own free will, while inconsistently recognising the values which condemn him. Our present age, Sartre tells us in an impressively pessimistic and eloquent passage, 'has a guilty conscience about history'. In the past, equally criminal societies did not care about posterity, while others made their history with a clear conscience, confident that they were creating a

secure future, at ease with the succession of gener-
ations. But now, 'revolutions are impossible', we are
threatened by annihilating war, propertied classes
have no confidence in their rights, and the working
class no confidence in its power. We are more aware of
injustice, without the will and the power to remove it.
The progress of science makes future centuries 'an
obsessive presence'. The future is here, we feel judged
by masked successors. Our age, which is already dead,
already a *thing*, though we still have to live through it,
is alone in history. What way is open to us, Sartre asks,
and replies that he can see one which he will discuss
elsewhere. This way is presumably that of the marriage of existentialism and Marxism which he allows
us to glimpse through the closing doors.

This book can serve as a picturesque link between
the metaphysic of *L'Être et le Néant* and that of the *Critique de la Raison Dialectique*. As an 'analysis' of the contradictions of bourgeois society, the futility of the
bourgeois subject, and the bankruptcy of bourgeois
morality, it professes to open a space for the new morality of existentialist Marxism, with its combination of
freedom and social change. Freedom is Genet's virtue,
the free activity of his own particular will, freedom as
unillusioned sincerity, freedom as courage. The book
is in effect a taking to extremes (I would say a *reductio
ad absurdum*) of both the earlier and the later views. As a
political tract it will fail to convince those who, though
they share Sartre's pessimistic fears, believe in traditional morality, and do not believe in a magical
transformation, effected by Marxism, or Marxism-
Existentialism, into a far better and totally different
society. The book, though so radiant with intelligence,
is equally unacceptable as a moral tract or adventure

in moral-philosophical psychology. Sartre says at the beginning that when he was with Genet 'we talked only about him'. 'I have a passion for understanding people,' Sartre adds. Perhaps Sartre, touchingly romantic about his hero, was too ready to accept Genet's view of himself which, encouraged by his admirer, he elaborated, too anxious also to see in Genet just those interesting characteristics which he perceived earlier in Baudelaire, later in Flaubert. Sartre claims that Genet never changed, never compromised with society by becoming merely 'a famous writer'; his 'verbal victory' did not separate him from his old haunts and companions, and his work never ceased to express his original scream of protest. Such generalisations, which tend to cut off further discussion, probably do less than justice to the paradoxical mysteriousness of Sartre's idol. Genet certainly writes like an angel and *Notre Dame*, in the extraordinary mix of that outpouring, contains intense images of love and tenderness, together with an effective, not merely scandalous, use of religious imagery. The contradictions within the talent make both man and writer more interesting. Sartre says that Georges Bataille's meditation upon images of suffering is 'a fake', whereas Genet's sado-masochistic visions are not fakes. Well, art is a sort of faking, the artist is and is not detached from the man, the influence is mutual. Genet is (to stir things by speaking wildly) like Christopher Isherwood, who also wrote like an angel, and like T. E. Lawrence, who was accused of 'faking' and whose life broods uneasily over his work. (Sartre mentions the *Seven Pillars* when seeking models for a book which Genet might have written but did not.) He is also of course, in his subject matter, his passion, his message, his history, tremendously unlike. There are interesting paradoxes, large reflections, which Sartre's determination to see Genet as a great unitary edifying object leaves unexplored. One would like, in this book, to be told in more heterogeneous detail about how Genet's private life related, as time went by, to the didactic 'moralism' of his art. Sartre gives us a 'touching' glimpse at the end of Genet 'surrounded by children', at the house of an ex-lover whose marriage he promoted and protects (dominates?). Sartre adds this interesting and ambiguous item, without further explanation, as an instance of Genet's generosity, and even remarks that homosexuals often develop 'artificial families' in middle age.

It is Genet the artist, the prose-master, the 'liberator' of the theatre, who will remain with us. His work poses the (very complex) problem of how far and how an artist's value judgements affect the worth of the work that expresses them. This used to be tamely discussed in relation to D. H. Lawrence. Sartre does not discuss it in the more striking case of Genet; and indeed cannot discuss it because he accepts Genet as an absolute and his literary work as something almost perfect. Be that as it may, Sartre's canonisation of Genet, in which the word 'evil' frequently occurs, seems devoid of any understanding of the reality of evil, the nature of cruelty, the harm done to its victims, the crippling (for instance the narrowing) of the evil-doer's mind, the spreading ripples of misery and further evil which evil acts produce. The actual operation of morality, its *variety*, which is the most obvious and ubiquitous feature of human existence, is absent from the picture. Sartre as Cartesian solipsist seems especially here to exhibit a lack of any lively sense of the mystery and contingent variousness of individuals, even of the individuality of his subject whom he presents with such dramatic simplicity. By now the metaphysician has said his final farewell to the messy accidental world of the novel, so full of encounters and moral conflicts and love.

The idea of 'existential psychoanalysis', first presented in *l'Être et le Néant*, underwent a lengthy development as Sartre made various attempts to apply it. Roughly, existential psychoanalysis differs from the Freudian variety in being less deterministic, and therein less scientific, in that it involves reference to the future as well as to the past. A philosophy of time belongs in a philosophy of man. Sartre never abandoned his original dictum that *l'homme se définit par son projet* which implies not only that man is free, but, more precisely, that a purposive conception of the future is always part of the present. The man of *l'Être et le Néant* possesses total freedom, there is no limit to his ability to leap out of his surroundings. As Sartre moved from this heady voluntarism toward Marxism he became more interested in the 'social conditioning' of the individual: a fairly obvious point of interest, one might say, to an observer of the human scene. Sartre ultimately became obsessed with this problem which he continually restated in its most abstract terms and then hastened to tackle in the utmost detail. The book on Flaubert is thus, as Sartre tells us in the preface, a sequel or appendix to the *Critique*, in particular to its long introduction *Questions de Méthode*. Its subject is: what can we know about a man today? Sartre will answer this question by studying a particular case, that of Flaubert. '*Cela revient à totaliser les informations dont nous disposons sur lui.*' The terrible verb to 'totalise', only recently becoming current in English, must be understood here with its full Hegelian aura. So, Sartre is to answer his extremely abstract and ambiguous question by some *total* examination and synthesis of *all* the available information about Flaubert. He admits that this may not be possible, perhaps the truth about an individual is essentially plural, the informative data being heterogeneous and irreducible. Sartre's book is to show that the mooted irreducibility is merely apparent, each piece of information set in its proper place will contribute to a whole, revealing its deep homogeneity with all the other items. Man is never really an individual, he is better described as a *universel singulier*: totalised and universalised by his epoch, which he retotalises by reproducing himself within it as a singularity. This picture of a man as totalisable, and totally intelligible to another man (albeit a very clever one) is a long way from the free solitary of the first synthesis, and smacks generally of determinism rather than freedom. Sartre is of course attempting the impossible, something he was often engaged in doing. The frailty of his operation is more frankly admitted in a later passage (p. 139), where he has been explaining the passive and 'pathetic' character of Flaubert's sexual relations by the fact that he was *mal aimé, bien soigné* by a mother who was conscientious but unloving. After many pages of details Sartre suddenly says, '*Je l'avoue: c'est une fable. Rien ne prouve qu'il en fut ainsi.*' 'I admit, it may be just a story. Nothing proves it was really like this.' The absence of the necessary details, the particular facts, necessitates recourse to generality. The account has reference to infants of a certain kind, not to Flaubert in particular. Never mind. Sartre has wanted to pursue his idea as thoroughly as possible because, even though the *real* explanation may be quite different, it would *have* to follow the same route as Sartre's and refute that of Sartre upon the same ground, which Sartre sums up as *le corps, l'amour*.

The Flaubert book is of course interesting as a very fully documented biography, but what Sartre is attempting to do with it cannot be done, partly for reasons which he mentions himself, the heterogeneous nature of the evidence, its dubious reliability, its lacunae, and also for more general reasons concerning the secret inaccessibility of other people and the fact that moral judgements are involved in assessing 'what they are'. The final judgement rests with common sense and moral sense: one cannot, however freneti-cally one tries, pluck out the heart of that mystery. I cannot help wishing that Sartre had devoted all that tremendous time-consuming energy to the writing of a 4000-page novel about everybody and everything. Long novels by geniuses are possibly the best totalisa-tions available. However, the attempt has what he must have felt to be its ineluctable *raison d'être* in the evolution of his politics. In the *Critique de la Raison Dia-lectique* Sartre observes, about another writer whose mystery intrigues him, 'Valéry is a petty-bourgeois intellectual, there is no doubt about that. But not every petty-bourgeois intellectual is a Valéry. The inad-equacy of the heuristic method of contemporary Marxism is contained in those two sentences.' Sartre's corrective 'proof,' which in the context of its preten-sions must appear as a *reductio ad absurdum*, was de-signed to discredit the abstract sociology of Marxism by a complete account of a man as a totality of social conditioning and personal *projet*. Sartre certainly satis-fied an existentialist ideal in that he lived his epoch to

the full. His conversion to Marxism and his adventures as a fellow-traveller dominated the second half of
his life, and elicited the ambitious second synthesis, in
which he attempts to revise or redeem Marxism by an
infusion of existentialism, a doctrine argued to be, as
compared with orthodox Marxism, closer to the ideas
of the early Marx. Of this large work only the first
volume was published, the promised second volume
existing only as a fragment. The industry of its author
is heroic, so is his sustained optimism, his lack of cynicism, and his faith in the role of philosophy. Marx
thought that philosophical speculation would disap-
pear in the good (communist) society. The young
Hegelian Marx was a kind of philosopher, the later
Marx more of a scientist. Orthodox western Marxism
had abandoned philosophy in favour of scientific
socialism. Sartre in both his incarnations remained a
traditional philosopher, thus giving his whole life to
philosophy, which remained fundamentally connected
with all his other writings. His least 'philosophical'
work is *Les Chemins*. In his second phase Sartre took it
as self-evident, a view shared with many Western
thinkers, that Marxism is *the philosophy* of the present-
day world. Marxism is taken to be, a word often used
by Sartre, *indépassable*. No other philosophy, it is
argued, is universally relevant, and universally intelligible and popular, and thus effective. It might I think
be suggested if one were searching for a global philosophy, that utilitarianism is a plausible candidate. Its
tenets are however instinctively rather than theoretically popular, and it may indeed be claimed as effectively part of Marxism, to the outsider probably the
most attractive part. Since 1945 an attempt has been
made, in various philosophical quarters, to revise

Marxism, to rescue it from its degeneration into pragmatic dogma and pseudo-science, and make of it a genuine living moral philosophy; which involves jettisoning the large quantity of 'philosophical' nonsense about dialectical materialism written by Engels and Lenin, and tolerating, excusing, or rejecting the claim of the Soviet Union to be a Marxist society. In France this rescue operation began earlier, in Paris in the 1930s, when Sartre, Merleau-Ponty and Raymond Queneau were listening to Alexandre Kojève's lectures on Hegel. It may be from this time that Sartre derived the idea of the close relation between existentialism and the Hegelianism of the young Marx, and so later came to believe that what was now necessary was to create a fusion of existentialism with Marxism, which had always really been an existentialist philosophy.

The introduction to Sartre's *Critique*, called *Questions de Méthode*, which was also published separately in *Temps Modernes*, summarises the problem and the theory. Sartre states firmly that he accepts *sans réserves* the dictum of Engels, in a letter to Marx, that 'men make their history themselves, but within a milieu which conditions them'. He adds that this text is not altogether clear, and is susceptible of many interpretations. How can man make history if history also makes man? Idealist Marxism, he goes on to say, has chosen the easiest interpretation: man, entirely determined by circumstances, in effect by economic conditions, is a passive product, a mere collection of conditioned reflexes. This puts the dilemma in its crudest and its clearest form. If Marxism is a science, a formulation of scientific law, it must appear as a kind of determinism, and this is how it is presented by

Engels when he explains that the human dialectic is really the same as the dialectical operation of the whole of nature. On the other hand, if Marxism is an economic theory designed to remove the contradictions of capitalism and produce a society without scarcity it seems more like a technological hypothesis; and if it is declared to be a philosophy it opens itself to heterogeneous free-for-all of speculation and admits of varying interpretations. In the last two forms, it lacks the absolute authority usually claimed for it by Marxists, and in the first form (as science) it is implausible and intolerable. How far Sartre remains from meeting these difficulties is suggested by the rather dreamy conclusion of the first part of his Introduction (called *Marxism and Existentialism*). Marxism is *indépassable*, we are told, so long as technical progress and changes in social relations have failed to free man from the burden of scarcity (*rareté*). Sartre refers us to Marx's reference to *cette époque lointaine*, that far-off time, when the reign of liberty will begin, when work is no longer imposed upon us by an external necessity and purpose. Then, Sartre says, 'when there will exist for *everyone* a margin of *real* freedom' (Sartre's italics) outside the mere production of material goods in order to support life, Marxism will have had its day, and a philosophy of freedom will take its place. 'But we have no means, no intellectual instrument, no concrete experience which enables us to conceive of that freedom and that philosophy.' This curious passage expresses the old Utopian Marxist confidence in the ability of Marxism to solve all human problems, postpones 'real freedom' (about which we can know nothing) until that *époque lointaine*, and proposes existentialist-Marxism, which reconciles determinism with an inferior kind of freedom, as *indé-*

passable for what must be seen as an interim period, during which our confidence in that philosophy, if it is still to be called Marxism, must depend on our belief in its practical success.

Marxism must be made to recognise the individual, the *aventure singulière* of human existence must be returned to the centre of the picture, history must be seen to be made by men. The individual life must be shown to be related to its historical surroundings, by a continuous to and fro *mediation* by various paths between the general and the particular, which would reveal the place and nature of free choice. The possibility of such a showing was to be proved by the work on Flaubert. Methods of mediation are to be sought out in the confused area of 'human studies' (psychology, anthropology, sociology) whose confusion must be clarified by relation to a 'totalising' philosophical base, and by the use of Marxist concepts by which alone the whole of history can be seen as that of individuals. Marx's analysis of the revolution of 1848 is taken here to serve as another model to prove that what is desired is also possible. However for all the weight of historical fact and historical analysis which it carries, the philosophical psychology of the *Critique* bears a ghostly resemblance to that of *L'Être et Le Néant*. Sartre has promised a new dialectic of subject and object, a return to Hegel, a reinstatement of human purpose and the union of theory and practice, ideas lost by the scientific materialism of the orthodox line. But he cannot get away from his original deep idea of the individual solitary and sovereign *consciousness*, his 'dialectic' pictures the ego confronting alien matter which it must dominate. Hegel's philosophy is after all a philosophy of consciousness, the *Phenomen-*

ology can be read as the story of a single mind. Sartre
attempts to see history as 'driven, not by scientific laws
or by an abstract inhuman super-purpose, but by
human willed purposes, so that its explanation and
being lies in a study of conscious human activity'. Such
a view could not please Marxists who wished to retain
the old sense of historical inevitability, or non-
Marxists who wished to do justice to contingency. In
Sartre's theory the contingent makes an appearance as
the *practico-inerte*, a practical inertia or inert practica-
bility of blind social forces; while, capable of overcom-
ing these, the larger sweep of history is displayed as
visibly influenceable by purposive groups of individuals. Such a view would leave Marxism in the position of a hypothesis, possibly productive of useful
regulative concepts. Sartre criticises Marxists for em-
phasising the pressure of past experience and reality,
but ignoring the influence of an imagined future, the
purposive *projet* characteristic of consciousness. He
boldly existentialises a prime Marxist tool by appropriating the idea of *praxis*, a concept which received its
Marxist definition in the *Theses on Feuerbach* (1845).
Praxis, by origin a Greek word meaning doing, trans-
action, practical activity, has in German, and also in
English, the general sense of practice as opposed to
theory. Sir Philip Sidney, quoted in the *Oxford English
Dictionary*, opposes it to *gnosis*, agreeing with Aristotle
that the fruit is praxis. Marx's theses, a set of eleven
brief statements, explain the difference between
Feuerbach's (and all other) materialism, and that of
Marx. Feuerbach pictures human beings, no longer
misled into religious or idealist 'other worlds', as individuals who are now free to contemplate the various
objects which make up this world. Marx says that

objective truth is not something waiting to be perceived by the static theoretical gaze of isolated persons, it is something which has to be made by the joint efforts of social beings, active not just in 'civil society' but in the new 'human society, or social humanity'. 'The philosophers have only *interpreted* the world in various ways; the point is to *change* it.' Marx's general point here may be seen as not only sound Hegelianism but sound sense. Theory is tested in practice. The relation of subject to object is not static but creative, dynamic (dialectical). Marx goes further, however, by defining his truth-seeking, or truth-making, as an exercise of power over the objective world which must ultimately take the form of 'revolutionary practice'. The word 'praxis' has by now become familiar in Marxist jargon meaning (roughly and often vaguely) revolutionary practical activity, a united theory-and-practice exerting a continual pressure upon historical events. Sartre complained that orthodox Marxism has now 'mechanised' this concept, meaning by it *de facto* work or *ad hoc* political action, whereas what it *ought* to mean was free, creative, inventive mind, the original spontaneous upsurge of the human consciousness which is continually creating the historical process. (Left-wing political discussion could profit from the removal of the word 'praxis', and the substitution in each case of an explanation in ordinary language.) Sartre's praxis-consciousness was, in the present scene, to appear as a group-purpose incarnate in the proletariat, the most alienated and rebellious section of society, and in the Communist Party as its fully conscious leader. Merleau-Ponty (in *Les Aventures de la Dialectique*) complained that Sartre had thus made of praxis a 'pure' activity, whose function was to produce a 'proletariat' which had no real existence, and was merely a figment representative of humanity in the thoughts of Sartre. '*Le je ne sais quoi Sartrien, la liberté radicale, prend possession de la praxis.*' Perhaps the invisible Spirit, mentioned in *Les Mots*, who was to save Sartre from chance, was never really exorcised after all.

It is impossible briefly to do justice to this huge ambitious book, full of very detailed exposition and excursions into anthropology and sociology as well as history, which was attacked by Marxist critics as abstract, idealist, Cartesian and a distraction from the realities of the political struggle. It is a less readable, and less felicitous or 'lucky' work than *L'Être et le Néant* whose spirit, I suggest, ineffectually animates it. The early book has a metaphysical unity and deeply felt and imagined central theme which this one lacks. *L'Être et le Néant* appeared as something new and appealed to an audience who were ready for it. The voluminous data which Sartre assembles in the *Critique* do not cohere together, the main argument is not comfortable with its numerous proofs and evidences, and the central ideas lack imaginative synthetic power. As a revision of Marxism it seems to me to be on the wrong road; the gallant attempt to join Marxism and existentialism fails, a *passion inutile*. Sartre was also, in the post-war period, very active in *ad hoc* day-to-day politics, in his journal *Temps Modernes* and in public political debate with critics such as Merleau-Ponty and Henri Lefebvre. He may not have been able to unite theory and practice, but he paid ardent attention to both. In spite of, or because of, his belief in the importance of the (or an ideal) Communist Party as a superconscious consciousness, he was never on easy terms

with the French Party. In the 'revolution' of 1968
Sartre was once more surrounded by the young people
whom he so much hoped to influence, but the moment
passed, no radical changes followed, and the Marxist
idea of the 'great transformation scene' was beginning
to fade. A question which divided, and still divides,
European communism was that of the leading political
role of the USSR, regarded by some as sacrosanct, by
others as a chief obstacle to rational Marxism. Sartre's
ambivalent position on this matter caused bitter arguments. On the one hand, the remarkable, indeed extraordinary, success of Lenin's party in 1917 could be
taken as a perfect example of purposive humans
making history. On the other hand, the USSR was not
a good society and other societies had not followed
suit. Many Marxists hesitated to criticise the Soviet
Union because to do so was to lend comfort to the
bourgeois enemy. Sartre may also have been
influenced by a kind of Hobbesian theoretical realism
which appears in the *Critique* in his views about the
effect of scarcity upon the nature of power. Violence is
(p. 221) *'L'inhumanité constante des conduites humaines en
tant que rareté interiorisée, bref ce qui fait que chacun voit en
chacun l'Autre et le principe du Mal.'* Scarcity 'interiorised'
leads every man to see his fellow as the Other, and as
the principle of Evil. *Homo homini lupus, l'enfer c'est les
autres.* Such a strongly expressed pessimism about
human nature might promote a realistic tolerance of
authoritarian government, in Russia, and, more plaus-
ibly, in China.

A general criticsm of the *Critique de la Raison Dialectique*, and which applies to much Marxist writing, is
that the factor of *morality* is, except in some extremely
diminished and reduced form, absent. Morality is after

all the great central arena of human life and the abode
of freedom. Almost all our thoughts and actions are
concerned with the infinitely heterogeneous business
of evaluation, almost all our language is value
language. The destruction or denial of this open
texture is and has been (as we know) the aim of many
theorists and many tyrannies. Moral (that is human)
activity can be controlled if it is conceptually simplified. The idea that we inevitably regard other people
not only as a nuisance but as prime founts of evil is certainly a simplification; and perhaps from a tyrant's
point of view not a very fruitful one, since a seed of individual will may be found within it. Sartre uses moral
terminology in a vague way when, in his analyses, he
speaks of 'oppression'; but the positive moral idea in
the *Critique* is, *mutatis* a few *mutandis*, the same as in
L'Être et le Néant, that of a world-dominating will.
Marxists who attacked the Soviet Union because of its
offences against human rights were angry with Sartre's
ambivalence in this matter. Axiomatic ideas about
human rights or natural rights are effective because
they do not belong to any system. The Kantian idea of
duty is individualised by conscience in particular contexts. General concepts such as Reason and Love are
instantiated in the cognitive activities of infinitely
various individuals. Morality is a very complicated
matter. This complication is dangerous to the simplified unity and fascination of political metaphysics. Religion is, *a fortiori*, not mentioned by Sartre except as a
sociological item. French anti-clericalism has always
been fierce and pointed, as compared with the vague
drift away from religion in other countries. Marxist
theoretical morality has usually appeared to consist of
(often reasonable) criticisms of bourgeois society, jux-

taposed with Utopian pictures of a better society (without 'alienation', class division, division of labour etc.). Such a theory certainly has a moral content, but a controlled and restricted one. The 'moral' of the *Phenomenology of Mind* might be said to be 'diligently seek truth'. Scientific socialism sets limits upon this appeal to the individual soul to enlarge itself. Marxist practice has of course been inspired by ideas of justice and utilitarian considerations which are not the exclusive property of Marxism. Even institutional Christianity, under the flag of the 'new theology', has, in South America, made friends with Marxism. The making of such alliances is an opportunistic tactic, but may also show that, in the field, the moral limitations of Marxism are not impenetrable. Officially however Marxists, pointing to the miseries of the world which Marxism will cure, tend to suggest or imply that while this general state of affairs exists all so-called (bourgeois) morality is self-indulgence and illusion. This is certainly a recognisable state of mind. Bourgeois value (morality) is something to be contrasted with (good) praxis and with the free blameless human relations which will exist in the *époque lointaine* when all contradictions are overcome and the burden of scarcity and necessary toil is laid down. Sartre offers his own theory of value along these lines in a footnote (p. 302) to the *Critique*. The ambiguity of all past and present morality is that it makes its appearance in a world of exploitation and oppression, a state of negation (of humanity) which morality then negates. Morality is thus a pseudo-positive, being a negation of a negation. In an oppressive society freedom can only assert itself through values but thereby is alienated. Every system of values rests on exploitation and oppression and confirms these, even the systems created by the oppressed do so in so far as they are systems. Value systems may be effective against *this* or *that* particular piece of oppression. But at the moment of revolution they cease to be systems and cease to be values, since their existence as such depended on structures which made them seem to be ultimate (*indépassable*) and which, being overthrown, reveal the values as otiose, as *significations depassées*. Freely developing praxis, as free creative consciousness, is then discovered as the only ethical relation between men as they proceed to dominate not each other but nature. (Presented with this version of the old old story the disenchanted may feel inclined to say that anyone who believes this will believe anything.) Sartre adds that Marxists tend to confuse value with talk about value. Value is produced at the level of basic praxis (that is, in Sartrian Marxism, purposive consciousness); and it is praxis itself, as relation of man to man and to worked matter, which is alienated, or not, and must be distinguished from the superstructures of value language and 'moralities' invented by intellectuals. Thus in the Soviet Union, moralistic talk, the utterance as values of moral generalities common to all, should not conceal or be confused with the collective praxis which is creating socialist society. This would seem to imply that the practice of, and inevitable talk about, bourgeois morality, that is ordinary morality, that is morality, is in some way false as contrasted with the silent real social relationships which are constitutive and creative of the good society. The notion that talk is false and only action is true (not unlike that of Wittgenstein in the *Tractatus*) can also be deduced from the psychology of *L'Être et le Néant*. Talk is *mauvaise foi*, choice reveals the man, and is the truth.

This is of course another simplification. Moral activity involves the human activity of language-using, even of theorising. 'Moralism' exists in the Soviet Union because, in spite of Marxism, ordinary morality exists there too, and would still do so even if the relations of production had been (which they have not been) radically altered and perfected.

Sartre's attempt to reform Marxism, and rid it of the naive deterministic dialectical materialism of Engels and Lenin, reads like a dream of history wherein scarcity, admitted to be a basis for unavoidable exploitation, disappears, and an enlightened proletariat leads mankind to a society where freedom itself will be the whole of value. Sartre retains, together with the familiar Marxist conceptual tools, the assumption that Marxism is (must be) a total systematic theory which explains and unifies everything. This quasi-religious claim, which has traditionally been made for Marxism, is tacitly or explicitly challenged now by many revisionists. Sartre had hoped to offer a synthesis which would not only explain the world (or explain how it could be explained), but would effect a revolution in Marxist thought which would gain popular support among intellectuals and activists. He hoped to influence *les jeunes*. He enjoyed the excitement of 1968, though disappointed by the failure of the French Communist Party to take charge of it. But his great work is now largely unread and revisionists look for inspiration elsewhere. The book which rallied the young was not the long one by Sartre but the short one by Marcuse. When one moves from the obsessive and over-wrought atmosphere of Sartre's second synthesis to the heterogeneous and mutually dissonant writings of the Frankfurt School one feels (however much disagreeing) that there is more open space and fresh air, more moral concepts, more realistic reflection. Practically, Marxism is held together by *de facto* tyranny and because it enshrines a political hope (or illusion); theoretically it may now be in process of a disintegration wherein out of loyalty, or dislike of other labels, all sorts of thinkers call themselves Marxists, and to adopt the title is a symbolic gesture. Sartre, for all that he was a heretic, was an optimist who believed that Marxism, only, could save civilisation. The thoughts of Adorno, Horkheimer and Benjamin make a different impression, sometimes even one of despair. We are told to look for the truth, not in the literary work of Sartre and Brecht, but in that of Kafka and Beckett. Is this the desolation of the bourgeois individual, or the desolation of man? Against the reified determinism of orthodox Marxists Sartre summoned up a subject-object dialectic whose slogan was 'all power to the subject'. Hegelianism lives so long as serious philosophical discussion can use its concepts. Adorno preaches the primacy of the object. Traditional Marxism pictures the strife of man with man as succeeded by a strife with nature, ultimately a domination of nature. Sartre's version pictures the world outside the *pour-soi* of pure praxis as an alien *en-soi* to be conquered by creative will. One may look back here, past *L'Être et le Néant*, to a *La Nausée*, whose hero looks out on a desert not unlike that conjured up by Beckett. Adorno's Hegelianism pictures knowledge as an attentive truthful patience with the contingent, where the latter is not a hostile Other to be overcome, but more like an ordinary world-round-about-us. 'Approaching knowledge of the object is the act in which the subject rends the veil it is weaving around the object. It can do this only where, fearlessly passive, it entrusts itself to its own experience. In places where subjective reasons scents subjective contingency the primacy of the object is shimmering through – whatever in the object is not a subjective admixture. The subject is the object's agent, not its constituent; this fact has consequences for the relation of theory and practice.' Yes, and one wonders if such a view is not destructive of a Marxist, or even Hegelian viewpoint. Adorno constantly denies the claim of any 'totality'. This picture of cognition which 'favours the object' also favours conceptions of truthfulness, of sacredness, of respect and duty and love which belong to ordinary traditional morality and might be more clearly expressed (as they are by Simone Weil) in ordinary-language reflections without the compulsory use of Hegelian-Marxist terminology. It suggests a philosophy better suited to a world in which respect for rights (human rights, rights of citizens, rights of blacks, rights of gays, rights of whales) has made innumerable places for the meeting of theory and practice.

Sartre rightly identified determinism as a prime enemy; and paradoxically out of the philosophical background which supplied Sartre with the 'structures' of his 'mediations', the new quasi-scientism, known as structuralism (or deconstructionism), has arisen. Languages of science and technology, 'deeper' than ordinary language, supply models for explanatory codes, easily simplified and popularised. Of course Derrida's structuralism exposes philosophical fallacies which were earlier the target of Wittgenstein, but its charms are those of determinism, pleasing to thinkers who exclude themselves from the fate of the codified. By contrast with a cosmos of *archiécriture*

Sartre may appear as a spokesman for the indomitable human spirit. A philosophy cannot be a total system because the world is contingent and infinitely various, and systematic philosophy is often made more readable as well as more reasonable by the personal interests of the philosopher, by the way in which his analyses and examples stray toward particular matters which have amazed him or frightened him or pleased him; so that his book may have turned out to be more personal and accidental than he intended. This is true of *L'Être et le Néant* and even, to a lesser extent, of the *Critique*. Sartre, thinker and artist, so versatile, so committed, so serious, industrious, courageous, learned, talented, clever, certainly 'lived' his own time to the full, and, whatever the fate of his general theories, must survive as one of its most persistent and interesting critics.

I

THE DISCOVERY OF THINGS

La Nausée[1] was Sartre's first novel, and it contains all his main interests except the political ones. It is his most densely philosophical novel. It concerns itself with freedom and bad faith, the character of the bourgeoisie, the phenomenology of perception, the nature of thought, of memory, of art. These topics are all raised as consequent upon a certain discovery, of metaphysical interest, which is made by the hero, Antoine Roquentin. This discovery, put in philosophical jargon, is the discovery that the world is contingent, and that we are related to it discursively and not intuitively.

Roquentin is standing on the sea shore. He has picked up a pebble which he is about to throw into the sea. He looks at the pebble—and a curious sickly horror overcomes him. He drops it and goes away. There follow other experiences of the same sort. A fear of objects invades him—but he cannot decide whether it is he or they that have changed. Looking at a glass of beer, at the braces of the café *patron*, he is filled with a 'sweetish sort of disgust' (*une espèce d'écoeurement douceâtre*). He looks at his own face in a mirror, and suddenly it seems to him inhuman, fishlike. He subsequently makes the discovery: *there are no adventures*. Adventures are stories, and one does not *live* a story. One tells it later, one can only see it from the outside. The meaning of an adventure comes from its conclusion; future passions give colour to the events. But when one is inside an event,

[1] Translated first into English under the title *The Diary of Antoine Roquentin*, and later as *Nausea*.

one is not thinking of it. One can live or tell; not both
at once. When one is living, nothing happens. There are
no real beginnings. The future is not already there.
Things happen, but not in the way that Roquentin had
liked to imagine when he believed in adventures. What
he had wanted was the impossible : that the moments
of his life should follow each other like those of a remembered life, or with the inevitability of the notes of a
familiar tune. He thinks, too, of his own work : he is
writing the life of the Marquis de Rollebon. Yet this
story which Roquentin is unravelling from letters and
documents is not the real life which Rollebon lived. If
he cannot even retain his own past, thinks Roquentin,
how can he save that of another? He sees it all in a
flash : the past does not really exist at all. There are the
traces, the appearances—and behind them nothing. Or
rather, what there is is the present, his own present—and
what is this? The 'I' that goes on existing is merely
the ever-lengthening *stuff* of gluey sensations and vague
fragmentary thoughts.

Roquentin visits the picture gallery, and looks at the
self-satisfied faces of the bourgeoisie. These people never
felt that their existences were stale and unjustified. They
lived surrounded by institutions of state and family, and
borne up by a consciousness of their own claims and
virtues. Their faces are *éclatant de droit*—blazing with
right. Their lives had a real *given* meaning, or so they
imagined; and here they are, with all that added sense of
necessity with which the painter's thought can endow
them. Roquentin's own recent experience has given him
a special sense of the bad faith of these attempts to
clothe the nakedness of existence with such trimmings of
meaning. *Salauds!* he thinks, as he returns to his own
nausée.

This *malaise* now moves towards a climax, and its

metaphysical character is made more clear. Roquentin is staring at a seat in a tramcar. ' I murmur : it's a seat, as a sort of exorcism. But the word remains on my lips : it refuses to go and rest upon the thing . . .' ' Things are delivered from their names. They are *there*, grotesque, stubborn, huge, and it seems crazy to call them seats or to say anything whatever about them.' He continues his reflections in the public park : though he has often said, for instance, ' seagull ', he has never before felt that *that* which he named *existed*. Before he had thought in terms of classes and kinds; now what is before him is a particular existing thing. ' Existence had lost the inoffensive air of an abstract category : it was the very stuff of things.' He fixes his eyes upon the root of a chestnut tree. Then comes the final and fullest revelation. ' I understood that there was no middle way between non-existence and this swooning abundance. What exists at all must exist to this point : to the point of mouldering, of bulging, of obscenity. In another world, circles and melodies retain their pure and rigid contours. But existence is a degeneration.'

Roquentin, who has abandoned his book on Rollebon, decides to leave. He sits in the café and listens for the last time to his favourite gramophone record : a Negress singing *Some of these days*. Often before, while listening to this melody, he has been struck by its pure, untouched, rigorous necessity. The notes follow one another, inevitably, away in another world. Like the circle, they do not exist. They *are*. The melody says : you must be like me. You must suffer in rhythm. I too, I wanted to *be*, thinks Roquentin. He thinks of the Jew who wrote the song, the Negress who sings it. Then he has another revelation. These two are *saved*, washed of the sin of existing. Why should he not be saved too? He will create something, a novel perhaps, which shall be beauti-

ful and hard as steel, and will make people ashamed of
their superfluity. Writing it, that will be a stale day to
day task. But once it is complete, behind him, he will
be thought of by others as now he thinks of the Jew and
the Negress. Some pure radiance from his work will fall
then upon his own past—and he will be able to recall his
past without disgust, and to accept it. With this resolution
of Roquentin's the novel ends.

This peculiar book lives on many levels. It is a sort of
palimpsest of metaphysical *aperçus*. It gives expression
to a pure metaphysical doubt, and also analyses that
doubt in terms of contemporary concepts. It is an
epistemological essay on the phenomenology of thought;
it is also an ethical essay on the nature of 'bad faith'.
Its moral conclusions touch aesthetics and politics. Most
of all, though, its power resides in its character as a
philosophical myth, which shows to us in a memorable
way the master-image of Sartre's thinking. Let us look
at these aspects one by one.

The metaphysical doubt which seizes Roquentin is an
old and familiar one. It is the doubt out of which the
problem of particularity and the problem of induction
arise. The doubter sees the world of everyday reality as
a fallen and bedraggled place—fallen out of the realm
of being into the realm of existence. The circle does not
exist; but neither does what is named by 'black' or
'table' or 'cold'. The relation of these words to their
context of application is shifting and arbitrary. What
does exist is brute and nameless, it escapes from the
scheme of relations in which we imagine it to be rigidly
enclosed, it escapes from language and science, it is more
than and other than our descriptions of it.

Roquentin experiences the full range of the doubt, and
he experiences it in a characteristically up-to-date way.
He feels doubts about induction (why not a centipede

for a tongue?) and about classification (the seagull), distress at the particularity of things and the abstractness of names (the tramway seat, the tree root). He sees reality as fallen and existence as an imperfection. He yearns for logical necessity in the order of the world. He wishes that he could know things through and through and experience them as existing necessarily. He wishes that he himself existed necessarily. He feels the vanity of these wishes. What Roquentin has in common with Hume and with present-day empiricists is that he broods descriptively upon the doubt situation, instead of moving rapidly on to the task of providing a metaphysical solution. Roquentin does not feel so sure that rational knowledge and moral certainty *are* possible; he examines piecemeal the process of thinking, the commonplaces of morality, and accepts the nihilistic conclusions of his study. A further result of his brooding over the doubt is the neurotic distress about language which then assails him; in this respect too Roquentin is of his age. But what marks him out as an existentialist doubter is the fact that he himself is in the picture : what most distresses him is that his own individual being is invaded by the senseless flux; what most interests him is his aspiration to *be* in a different way.

Roquentin's sensations are not in themselves so rare and peculiar. We all of us experience, for instance, that sense of emptiness and meaninglessness which we call *ennui*. In so far as Sartre exaggerates in Roquentin our ordinary feelings of boredom and loss of meaning this is in order to bring home to us a point which ' carelessness and inattention' usually obscure. What is a thought? asks Sartre, and attempts a reply which, like that of Professor Ryle, surprises us in proportion to its exactness. It is bodily feelings, it is words that surge up and vanish, it is a story I tell myself later. When we look at it closely, meaning vanishes—as when we repeat a word over and over, or stare at our faces in a mirror. If we consider our lives from moment to moment we observe, as Roquentin does, how much of the sense of what we are doing has to be put in afterwards. We observe the fabricated and shifting character of our memories. Meaning vanishes—yet we have to restore it.

In doing so, can we avoid lying? Roquentin asks himself. This is one of the central questions of the book. His acute feeling of the breakdown of meaning makes him look with clairvoyant amazement upon the bourgeoisie, past and present, of the town where he is living. He observes, with a fury which echoes the *belle haine* of his author, the pretentious trappings of the bourgeois Sunday. These trappings, these ideas of law and right, hide the nakedness of reality, of existence. But could one ever do without the trappings? To be outside society, to have lost one's human dignity, often appears to have for Sartre a positive value. Gauguin and Rimbaud are minor saints in the existentialist calendar for this reason. To have ' gone away ', literally or spiritually, from the rest of humanity may be at least a step away from bad faith, towards sincerity. Roquentin, when he is enlightened, feels himself to have lost his role as a social human being. He might, he feels, do anything. It is important that Roquentin has no *être-pour-autrui*, no close connexion with other people and no concern about how they view him; it is partly this that enables him to be such a pure case. His only confidante is his former mistress, Anny, who is his *alter ego*. Roquentin's introspections have, as a result of his loneliness, a peculiar purity. His temptations to play-act are reduced to a minimum. The conclusions of his analysis, however, seem to be fairly negative ones. What he learns is this. We must live forwards, not backwards. Not only every generation

but every moment, is ' equi-distant from eternity '. We
are not to live with our eye on History or on our biographer—to do so involves us in *mauvaise foi* and
destroys the freshness and sincerity of our projects. As
language may solidify and kill our thoughts, so our values
may be solidified if we do not subject them to a continual
process of breaking down and re-building. This much
is implicitly suggested by the analysis—but Sartre does
not explain or examine it. *La Nausée* offers no clear
answer to the ethical problems which it raises. It reads
more like a corrective, a sort of hate poem—whose negative moral is : ' only the *salauds* think they win ', and its
positive moral : ' if you want to understand something
you must face it naked.'

Yet Roquentin does finally resolve the doubt; or at any
rate he finds a means of personal deliverance from the
curse of existing. Roquentin is a Platonist by nature. His
ideal mode of being, to which he often recurs in thought,
is that of a mathematical figure—pure, clear, necessary
and non-existent. The little tune, in which the notes die
willingly one after the other, also has a kind of necessity
—and it is through the little tune that Roquentin finds
his rather dubious salvation. He thinks of the Negress
and the Jew who created it as having been somehow
saved by the song. Their salvation does not lie, presumably, simply in their being thought about by others—
if this were salvation then Herostratus is saved too.
(Herostratus set fire to the temple of Diana at Ephesus
in order to be remembered. Sartre studies a modern
version of this character in *Le Mur*.) Nor are they saved
because they have created a great work of art; Sartre
chooses *Some of these days* as the vital song partly no
doubt for this reason, that it is *not* a great achievement.
What then is the salvation which Roquentin hopes for?
We have to work this out from one or two obscure

phrases at the very end. 'A moment would come when the book would be written, would be behind me, and I think that a little of its radiance would fall upon my past. Then perhaps through it I could remember my life without disgust. . . I should be able, in the past, only in the past, to accept myself.'

Others have hoped for salvation through art: Virginia Woolf, who attempts 'to make of the moment something permanent' by finely embalming it; Joyce, who tries to change life itself into literature and give it the cohesion of a myth; Proust who seeks by reminiscence to bind up and catch in the present the stuff of his own past. What Roquentin here proposes to himself seems different from any of these. He does not imagine that while writing his novel he will experience any sense of justification or escape from absurdity. Nor does he think that he can rest upon having written it—*being* an author. To do this would be to fall into the very traps which he has himself exposed elsewhere—to attempt to catch time by the tail. It is rather that through the book he will be able to attain to a conception of his own life as having the purity, the clarity and the necessity which the work of art created by him will possess. This is what I take Sartre to mean by 'the radiance falling on the past'. Yet this is a very thin and unsatisfactory conclusion. A novel *may* be thought of as aspiring to the condition of a circle—though the comparison seems less suitable here than in the case of any other art. It certainly may be thought of as conferring upon an image of life and character a certain tense self-contained form, a sort of internally related necessity. But how is Roquentin, the creator, to transfer these yearned-for properties to, even, his own past? If no present thoughts of his own can confer necessary form upon his past, then neither can a partial image of that past, worked up into the wholeness

of a work of art, confer the necessity. Any such sense
of necessity must be illusory, for reasons which Roquentin has been offering all through the book. The best
which he could hope would be to achieve a momentary
sense of justification by contemplating the formal beauty
of his novel and saying to himself very rapidly: 'I did
that'.

The interest of *La Nausée* does not lie in its conclusion,
which is merely sketched in; Sartre has not developed
it sufficiently for it even to pose as a solution to the
problem. Its interest lies in the powerful image which
dominates it, and in the descriptions which constitute
the argument. These evocations of the viscous, the fluid,
the paste-like sometimes achieve a kind of horrid poetry,
calling up in the reader—as do so many passages in the
work of Sartre—*une espèce d'écoeurement douceâtre*, the
sweetish sort of disgust which is one form of *la nausée*
itself. Yet the effect is not always unpleasant. Sartre is
much concerned with the real nature of perception. He
dwells on the interpenetration of sensible qualities and
on the unlikeness of what we 'really see' to our dried-up
concept of the visible world. We are invited to redis-
cover our vision. The things which surround us, usually
quiet, domesticated and invisible, are seen suddenly as
strange, seen as if for the first time. The result may be
disconcerting and surrealistic, and it may be impressive
too. 'The real sea is cold and black, full of creatures;
it crawls beneath that thin green film that is made to
cheat us.' The vision of the phenomenologist has something in common with that of the poet and the painter.

What kind of book is *La Nausée*? It seems more like
a poem or an incantation than a novel. We find its hero
interesting, but we do not find him particularly touching.
Sartre says in *L'Etre et le Néant* that pure introspection
does not reveal character. Roquentin is depicted as so

lacking in the normal vanities and interests of a human being as to be rather colourless. Even his sufferings do not move us, for he himself is not their dupe. The solidity and colour of *La Nausée* are as it were cast out of Roquentin's excessively transparent consciousness on to the things that surround him. The transparent hero in the absurd world reminds us of the work of Kafka. But *La Nausée* is not a metaphysical tale, like *The Castle*, nor is the absurdity of Sartre the absurdity of Kafka. Kafka's K. is not himself a metaphysician; his actions show forth, but his thoughts do not analyse, the absurdity of his world. The hero of *La Nausée* is reflective and analytical; the book is not a metaphysical image so much as a philosophical analysis which makes use of a metaphysical image. This, its consistently reflective, self-consciously philosophical character, is what distinguishes it too from other novels which brood equally upon the senseless fragmentation of our experience or on the fabricated nature of its apparent sense: Virginia Woolf displaying the idle succession of moments, Proust telling us that what we receive in the presence of the beloved is a negative which we develop later, Joyce piling up details until no story contour is visible any more.

Kafka's K. persists in believing that there is sense in the ordinary business of human communication. His world is full of pointers which the hero feels bound to attend to, and to which he attends forever hopefully, although it always seems that in the end they point nowhere. In all his activities he hopes for sense, without anywhere cornering it. Sartre's hero, after his enlightenment, no longer seeks for sense anywhere except in the one place where he *knows* it resides, that is in the intelligibility of melodies and mathematical figures. He is unmoved by the fact that these are man-made fictions; it is their pure form which rescues them from absurdity.

Roquentin's plight appears to be a philosopher's plight, while K.'s is that of everyman. We do not in fact resign ourselves to finding the everyday world a senseless place —but in so far as we find it harder and harder to make sense of certain aspects of it, we recognise K.'s dilemma as our own.

Roquentin's problem is not the usual human problem. He is incurably metaphysical by temperament and lives totally without human relations. But nevertheless Sartre does, I think, intend to offer us here an image of the human situation in general. What he undoubtably does succeed in displaying to us is the structure of his own thought. *La Nausée* is Sartre's philosophical myth. Why, asks Gabriel Marcel, does Sartre find the contingent over-abundance of the world nauseating rather than glorious? What is, for him, the fundamental symbol?

In *L'Etre et le Néant* (the chapter called *Quality as Revealing Being*) Sartre discusses the fascination of the viscous. He describes it as ' an existential category, immediate and concrete'. It is one of the fundamental keys or images in terms of which we understand our whole mode of being, and its sexual character is merely one of its possible determinations. It fascinates us from the start, because it serves as an image of our consciousness, of the very form of our appropriation of the world. The metaphors which compare the mind to gluey manifestations of the sensible are not mere figures of adult fancy, they represent categories which we have used from earliest childhood. Sticky substances alarm and fascinate us, and we enjoy discovering and filling cavities, not originally for the reasons the Freudians offer, but because we grasp these as even more general categories of being: the consciousness that seeks to rise freely towards completeness and stability is continually sucked back into its past and the messy stuff of its moment-to-moment experience.

Roquentin reveals the human situation in a simplified mythological way. His aspiration follows the schematic pattern which Sartre has analysed in *L'Etre et le Néant* as the ground plan of all endeavour. It has not clothed itself in any form of normal human project, sexual, political, or religious. The aesthetic determination which is adopted at the very end is simply a sketch of a solution, the most abstract possible, which leaves the pattern unchanged. For Roquentin all *value* lies in the unattainable world of intelligible completeness which he represents to himself in simple intellectual terms; he is not (until the end) duped into imagining that *any* form of human endeavour is adequate to his yearning to rejoin that totality. 'Evil', says Sartre in *What is Literature?*, 'is the irreducibility of man and the world of Thought.' This indeed is Roquentin's evil, the only one which he recognises—as intelligible being is the only good which he recognises. *La Nausée* represents the naked pattern of human existence, illuminated by a degree of philosophical self-consciousness that reveals the fruitlessness which the particular determinations of our projects usually obscure.

How does Sartre intend us to understand his myth? He is patently uninterested in the aesthetic solution. Nor, although Roquentin indulges in a certain amount of political analysis, does he seriously consider a political solution. He observes with disgust the ossified rigidity of bourgeois convention—but the pure radiant life with which the little melody is endowed never appears to him capable of assuming the form of a political end. The anti-rationalist, anti-essentialist teachings of the book, though they sometimes provide negative arguments against çapitalism, or, more generally, institutionalism and bureaucracy, never take on a more positive ideological character.

Fully to understand *La Nausée* we must look elsewhere in Sartre's work; the questions which it raises are all to receive their answers later. Elsewhere a more positive note is struck, and we are shown, not the bare abstract pattern of the human situation in general, but a situation which bears the colour of Sartre's own projects. In *La Nausée*, however, we are still at the abstract level. *La Nausée* is the instructive overture to Sartre's work. To what extent it offers us an adequate picture of human consciousness I shall discuss later. What it certainly does give us is a powerful presentation of Sartre's own fundamental metaphysical image.

II

THE LABYRINTH OF FREEDOM

Les Chemins de la Liberté consists of four novels, *L'Age de Raison* (*The Age of Reason*), *Le Sursis* (*The Reprieve*), *La Mort dans l'Ame* (*Iron in the Soul*) and *La Dernière Chance*. The first three have appeared in English under the titles given in parentheses. The promised fourth, *La Dernière Chance*, was not completed, but an important fragment of it appeared in Sartre's review *Les Temps Modernes* for November and December 1949. *L'Age de Raison* chiefly concerns the search of the hero Mathieu for the price of an abortion for his mistress, Marcelle. The events described take place in 1938. *Le Sursis* is about the Munich crisis, and *La Mort dans l'Ame* about the fall of France. The story, which portrays the same group of characters throughout, follows straight on through the three books.

Les Chemins is a study of the various ways in which people assert or deny their freedom in that pursuit of stable fullness of being, or self-coincidence, which Sartre has said in *L'Etre et le Néant* to be characteristic of human consciousness and which he portrayed in *La Nausée*. Only whereas in *La Nausée* we are shown abstractly the empty form of the human project, *Les Chemins* attempts to show us concretely a variety of the ways in which different people try to realise it. Sartre studies at length what he considers to be three main types of consciousness, that of the ineffective intellectual (Mathieu), the pervert (Daniel), and the Communist (Brunet)—and introduces a host of minor characters who are also analysed and ' placed '.

The simplest of the three main cases is that of Daniel.

Daniel, like Roquentin, is tormented by the elusiveness of his own existence. He is obsessed with a desire to change the not-being of his consciousness into a stable thing-like being. A tendency which, if Sartre's description is the appropriate one, we all share, is found in Daniel as a constant and self-conscious preoccupation. Daniel is like Roquentin and unlike the other characters in *Les Chemins* in that he sees his life not as a pursuit of a variety of ordinary human ends, but as a single project whose content may change but whose form never varies. Reflexion strips his life to an awareness of a certain persistent structure. Yet whereas Roquentin, amid the raw material of metaphysical discovery, maintains a colourless philosophical detachment, the same discovery made by Daniel appears as a neurosis. Daniel is Roquentin, with the metaphysical thirst changed into an obsession, and the philosophical detachment into a flair for psychoanalysis. Daniel's story reads more like a Freudian case history than like a metaphysical essay.

Daniel wishes ' to *be* a pederast, as an oaktree is an oaktree'. Yet he is never able to *experience* a pure coincidence with his vice; he remains detached from it, an observer, a possibility. His attempts to achieve coincidence take the form of self-punishment. By this means he hopes to gain an intense identification of the tormentor and the tormented within himself. This sort of partial suicide will be, at the same time, a manifestation of freedom. To do the opposite of what one wants—that, he tells himself and Mathieu, is freedom. It is also self-coincidence, the striking down, even for a moment, of the winged elusive consciousness. Thus, paradoxically, one could *will* one's transmutation into a thing, and *be* just one quivering moment of pain. Daniel finds freedom in its opposite.

Yet his attempts at self-torment disappoint him. He

cannot bring himself to drown his cats. He marries Marcelle, whom he detests, and finds the marriage intolerably bearable. In search of a witness before whom he may experience the pleasant shame of being *seen* as a contemptible object he makes confessions to Mathieu. But Mathieu is too reasonable and tolerant to be a suitable witness. Daniel finds a better solution in religious experience. He is suddenly pierced by the certainty that God sees him. Here at last is a witness before whom all his vices exist really, solidified into things by the accusing gaze; but this too is evidently only one more phase in his endless quest. In Volume III (at the fall of Paris) he encounters what appears to be the perfect partner, the self-tormenting boy Philippe, who is drawn closely from Sartre's conception of Baudelaire—a conception which he has set out at length in his ' existential psychoanalytical' study of the poet. Daniel ' captures ' the youth and prepares them both for collaboration.

These studies are accurate and powerful. Sartre is undoubtedly a connoisseur of the abnormal; yet his interest therein is not necessarily a morbid one. Sartre, like Freud, finds in the abnormal the exaggerated forms of normality. His more lurid characters are to show us, either by direct analysis (Daniel) or half-symbolically (Charles), something of the *malaise* of the human spirit in face of its freedom. Like Freud too, Sartre uses a mythology or picture of the mind in terms of which the individual case may be described. But as a psychoanalyst he remains impenitently Cartesian. In his early *Essay on the Emotions* Sartre writes : ' The deep contradiction in all psychoanalysis is to present at once a relation of causality and a relation of comprehension between the phenomena it studies.' What occurs in the consciousness, he says, can receive its explanation only from the consciousness. Psychological abnormality must be understood in terms of the subject's own choice of a 'mode' of appropriating the world, and the subject's own purposefully sustained symbolism.

So where a Freudian might say that Daniel's guilt feelings at his homosexuality *cause* him to punish himself, Sartre puts the matter in terms of Daniel's semi-deliberate project, his chosen mode of life. That it is chosen is something which Daniel realises, and the realisation is a characteristic part of his torment. The subject is the final arbiter, Sartre argues, and this the practising psychoanalyst well knows, although he tends to forget it when he enters his study to theorise. Sartre thus rejects the idea of the unconscious mind, but has his own substitute for it in the notion of the half-conscious, unreflective self-deception which he calls 'bad faith' (*mauvaise foi*). As metaphysician, as moralist and as psychoanalyst Sartre works with the same tools; a single picture of the mind serves him in all his fields. Since freedom is fundamental there is no clash between psychoanalysis and morality; since metaphysics studies the structure of our experience of the world we need not be surprised to find a case history figuring as part of a philosophical argument.

A second meaning-problem is presented in the character of Brunet, the Communist. Whereas Daniel, with neurotic self-consciousness, pursues a form of achievement whose content is never constant, Brunet unreflectively identifies himself with a single concrete project. Throughout the first two volumes, and most of the third one, Brunet is the simple dogmatic Party member. The universe solidly and reassuringly *is* as the Marxist analysis says it is. He himself *is* an instrument of the Party whose function has been determined by History. Brunet reflects no more about these things; he acts. He does not even pause to rehearse or question his own motives for being in the Party. 'I'm a Communist because I'm a Communist, that's all.' Brunet, whose later development is so important, remains throughout the earlier part of *Les Chemins* a rather stick-like character, though one who is clearly liked and respected by his author.

The pivot of the first three volumes, the central image of the triptych, is Mathieu, the most expansively introspective of the psychoanalytical observers through whom the story is told, and no doubt a portrait of Sartre himself. Mathieu stands between the deliberately fallen and perverted nature of Daniel and the naïvely but innocently engaged nature of Brunet. Both these characters ' tempt' Mathieu in typical ways—Daniel with the prospect of an *acte gratuit*, Brunet with that of a secure engagement. When Daniel suggests to Mathieu that he (Mathieu) should marry Marcelle, he is not only attempting sadistically to harm his friend, he is offering a programme of salvation of a kind which he has just tried to carry out himself (the attempt to drown his cats) and which he subsequently does carry out (by his own marriage to Marcelle). 'It must be very amusing deliberately to do the opposite of what one wants. One feels oneself becoming another person.' Brunet also has a programme to offer Mathieu: join the Communist Party. 'You have renounced everything to be free. Take one more step, renounce your liberty itself: and everything will be given back to you.'

Mathieu, however, follows the advice of neither. He is paralysed by his excessive lucidity; there is no *reason* why he should go to Spain, or marry Marcelle, or join the C.P. For him to be able to decide he would have to change ' to the marrow of his bones '. As it is, he is an empty thought, reflecting on itself. Nowhere in his too rational life is there an irrevocable decision; ' the consequences of my actions are stolen from me.' When he does act it is Hamlet-like, on the spur of the moment, without any marshalling of reasons. He plants the knife in his hand to please Ivich. He opens his mouth to say ' I love you ' to Marcelle, and says ' I don't love you.' He tells Pinette that resistance is senseless, and then takes a rifle.

The climax of Mathieu's story is told in Volume III. Mathieu is a private in the defeated French Army which, deserted by its officers, awaits capture by the Germans. The description of this queer interval, where guilt and innocence are found unexpectedly together, achieves a sort of poetry which is not apparent elsewhere in *Les Chemins*. A strange profundity and gentleness attend the soldiers as they stroll about, smiling to one another. Mathieu thinks, this is the paradise of despair—and he wonders, as some stranger gently salutes him, ' must men have lost everything, even hope, for one to be able to read in their eyes that man could conquer?' Here the philosophy is completely fused with the image constituted by the story. Mathieu's musings no longer seem like interludes. A real emotion binds the tale together, and the self-consciousness of its hero no longer has a chilling and detaching effect.

Between Mathieu's *coup de tête* in joining the suicide squad of resisters and the final climax in the bell tower, the hero has time to ask himself one more question, as he looks down towards the cellar where his unheroic comrades lie drunk. Ought he not to be down there, not up here? ' Have I the right to drop my friends? Have I the right to die for nothing?' He has one final moment of illumination as he fires from the tower. ' He approached the parapet and began to shoot, standing up. It was an immense retribution; each bullet revenged him for a former scruple. . . he fired on man, on Virtue, on the World: Liberty is Terror.' There is no doubt that here the author is speaking. Into this symbolic irresponsible 'breaking of the plates' Sartre throws himself with an equal zest, as he hurls his hero to a senseless destruction.

While Mathieu is on a tower, Brunet is in a cellar. Mathieu was in perpetual doubt and casts himself away without a reason. Brunet is never in doubt, and nurses himself for future tasks. In the prison camp he appears as almost a caricature of the hard party bureaucrat— until he is warmed into life by Schneider. This mysterious person, gentle, humane and sceptical, is the critic both of Brunet's practical attitude to his fellows and of his confident rendering of the Party line. Volume IV opens with the unmasking of Schneider as a distrusted ex-Party member, and the discrediting of Brunet's interpretation of Party policy. But now he is full of doubts; for the first time he begins to have thoughts which do not belong to the Party, he begins to see the Party from the outside. Supposing U.S.S.R. fights and is beaten? Supposing the Party is wrong? 'If the Party is right, I am more lonely than a madman; if the Party is wrong, all men are alone and the world is done for.' Finally Brunet attempts an escape with Schneider. They are discovered and Schneider is shot. 'No human victory can efface this absolute of suffering : the Party has killed him, even if U.S.S.R. wins, men are alone.'

The book is an argument, proceeding by an alternate use of pointed symbolism and explicit analysis. It opens with Mathieu's encounter with the drunken beggar who intended to go to Spain but never got there. Mathieu remembers him at the close of Volume I. Mathieu too had intended to go to Spain, to join the Communist Party, to marry Marcelle. The sort of act which Mathieu *can* perform is typified in his planting the knife in his hand, which he remembers later when he is on the bell tower. The *typo*'s leap to death from the railway wagon (also killed by the Party) prefigures the death of Schneider, and gives Brunet his first taste of the irrevocable. Analysis is more important, however. Most of what Sartre has to say to us is, we feel, packed into the lengthy passages of introspective musing. The characters (particularly Daniel and Mathieu) become transparent to us; their cool intellectual probings both interest us and check our emotion. Like Marcelle, we begin to long for *un petit coin d'ombre*. Too much of the story is predigested for us in the consciousness of the main characters—and we too soon begin to know what to expect from each. Their reflexions, instead of deepening our sense of their concreteness and complexity, strip them to the bare structure of the particular problem which they embody.

In the relations of the characters to each other there seems to be no middle point between the insight of the analyst and being completely at a loss. Mathieu and Daniel observe each other with a professional shrewdness; in his relations with Marcelle, and even more with Ivich, Mathieu is totally confused. For all the subtlety of the analyses of our consciousness of others which Sartre offered us in *L'Etre et le Néant*, the ' other ' appears in *Les Chemins* either as a case or as a secret. Boris and Ivich, the faintly sinister and clam-like brother and sister, represent a value before which the protagonists (and their author) hesitate, but which they do not engage with or explore.

Ivich is a living reproach to Mathieu, yet one which he (and, one feels, his author) fails to understand. The value which Ivich represents is that of the secret, the inward, the momentary, the irrational—in the presence of which Mathieu can only feel embarrassment. In the

absence of any real communication the other person is
metamorphosed into an alarming enigma, even a Medusa.
But Mathieu's isolation, the drama of which we may
accept in his relations with Ivich, appears, where his
relations with Marcelle are concerned, as a sort of casual-
ness or carelessness on the part of the author. Mathieu
is seen as alternating between a dogged absorption in
events and glimpses of his ' freedom ', which he pictures
as a sort of grace, a sort of crime, and which bids him
simply to drop Marcelle. Sartre has not troubled to
see the relation between Mathieu and his mistress. What
interests him, and Mathieu, is not Marcelle's plight at
all, but an abstractly conceived problem of which her
plight is the occasion.

Sartre by-passes the complexity of the world of ordinary human relations which is also the world of ordinary
moral virtues. Oreste in *Les Mouches* remarks that
' human life begins on the other side of despair '. It
begins with the denuding experience of a radical reflexion. Till then, all is bad faith. The primary virtue is
sincerity. In *Les Chemins* we constantly feel the violent
swing from a total blindness to a total freedom, from
the silence of unreason to an empty and alarming babble
of reflexion. Human life *begins*. But the complexity of
the moral virtues, which must return, more deeply apprehended perhaps, with the task of ' going on from there ',
this we are not shown. Sartre takes his heroes up to the
point of insight, realisation, despair—and there he leaves
them. They may fall back, but they do not know how
to go on. There is only one hint of deep commitment,
of real emotion, in the personal sphere, and that is in
the relationship of Brunet and Schneider—and here one
feels that the *gaucherie* and embarrassment of Brunet
are somehow shared by his author. There is the touch
of an intensity which remains unanalysed. The waters

are troubled. But Schneider perishes and it was after all, as Sartre entitles it in *Les Temps Modernes, un drôle d'amitié.*

The more we look at *Les Chemins* the more the fundamental pattern which emerges is the same as that of *La Nausée.* All human communion is impure and opaque, and reflexion dissolves it without purifying it. Fruitless and precarious cogitation is the alternative to a descent into the meaningless. The loss of sense in human relations is asserted rather than displayed; there is no tormenting entanglement of misunderstanding between Sartre's characters. They bump into each other in an external fashion; they are deeply involved with each other. If not analysed they remain impenetrable. We are touched indeed by a fear of the senseless, but it takes a different form. In *La Nausée* it attended the hero's awareness of the crowded superfluity of *things.* In *Les Chemins* it appears rather as a horror of the flesh. The flesh symbolises the absolute loss of freedom, and references to its inertness, flabbiness, stickiness, heaviness form a continual accompaniment to the narrative. Mathieu's distress presents itself to us not as a spiritual involvement with Marcelle, but as a sheer horror of her pregnancy.

Yet what is it to defeat senselessness? To find some comment on this we may look at Mathieu's adventures in Volume III. There is, first, the intuition of a possible innocence, a possible human victory, which comes with the complete loss of hope. Touching as this is, it comes to Mathieu simply as a vague and sentimental nostalgia, with no clear significance. Then there is the question: have I the right to die for nothing? This is what the existentialist martyr asks himself. What sort of losing of one's soul will save it? Kierkegaard once asked himself if any man had the right to die for religion; but the background of Kierkegaard's question is a transcendent religious truth. Mathieu's question has no background. It simply expresses his sense of the absurdity of his act, and his refusal to regard it as a ' better thing ' than seeking safety in the cellar. He has had his nostalgic intuition of a purity and human communion which he never found in experience. But his final achievement lies in sheer violence, and what he achieves is simply the density and completeness of action which excludes reflexion. ' Liberty is terror.' This is the final ' going away ', the final ' losing of oneself '; this is, in a thin disguise, the old familiar romantic answer to the problem.

It is clear that Sartre is attached to this answer—the zest of Mathieu's dying speech is unmistakably personal. But it is not the one which he is responsibly anxious to endorse. To see the sketch of what this may be, we must look at the other emotional climax of the work, the death of Schneider. 'No human victory can efface this absolute of suffering.' Here too there is the same sense of a ' paradise lost '—a paradise of human companion-ship—and of a final isolation. But here something more is affirmed, namely that the moment of human love had its absolute value, that its loss is an absolute loss. In contrast to the Marxists, Sartre may appear as a moralist of a Christian type. His theological and his philosophical ancestry (Pascal on the one hand and Descartes on the other) come together in his view of the individual con-sciousness as an absolute. It is on the lonely awareness of the individual and not on the individual's integration with his society that his attention centres. In Sartre's world rational awareness is in inverse ratio to social integration; as soon as his characters begin to reflect they detach themselves from their background. Only the unreflective and implicitly condemned ' bourgeois ' (Jacques Delarue for instance) is depicted as socially at home. There is no social context which is blameless and which increased awareness does not disrupt. But neither is there any stability in relationships on the personal plane. The Christian philosopher Marcel broods upon the tenacity and reality of human communion in the midst of its obscurities and perversions. Here by contrast Sartre shows as a non-Christian thinker. The individual is the centre, but a solipsistic centre. He has a *dream* of human companionship, but never the experience. He touches others at the fingertips. The best he can attain to is an intuition of paradise, *un drôle d'amitié*.

III

THE SICKNESS OF THE LANGUAGE

Sartre says: 'The function of a writer is to call a spade a spade. If words are sick, it is up to us to cure them. . . If one starts deploring the inadequacy of language to reality, like Brice Parain, one makes oneself an accomplice of the enemy, that is, of propaganda . . . I distrust the incommunicable; it is the source of all violence.'[1]

What is this sickness of the language? It is impossible to give a neat answer to the question. The fact is that our awareness of language has altered in the fairly recent past. We can no longer take language for granted as a medium of communication. Its transparency has gone. We are like people who for a long time looked out of a window without noticing the glass—and then one day began to notice this too. The beginnings of this new awareness lie far back (in England, one may find it in Hobbes and Locke) but it is only within the last century that it has taken the form of a blinding enlightenment or a devouring obsession. The more one looks at the phenomenon the more one has that feeling of discovery which is made in all spheres simultaneously; the sort of feeling which tempts people to invoke the useless notion of the *Zeitgeist*. One suddenly begins to connect *The Concept of Mind* with the marble sugar lumps of surrealism (attacks on the notion of essence) and Hegel's *Logic* with *Finnegans Wake* (attempts to present the universe con-

[1] *What is Literature?* pp. 210-11. Quotations from *What is Literature?* are taken from Bernard Frechtman's translation. All other translations quoted are my own.

cretely and non-discursively as one huge pulsating interpenetrating particular).

This age may or may not deserve to be called one of 'existentialist' thinking, but it is certainly the ending of a period of 'essentialist' thinking. In every sphere our simple 'thingy' view of the world is being altered and often disintegrated at an unprecedented rate; and a crisis in our view of the operation of language is inevitable. This fragmentation may sometimes appear as the pure joy of a new discovery, a more exact observation. It was with no sense of loss that Monet declared that the principal person in a picture was the light. In the delighted vision of the impressionist painter the world of hard self-contained objects was transformed into a scintillating haze of 'appearances', a dance of 'sense data'. This was done too in the name of a new realism, an observation which, set free from the stale domination of 'essences' and general notions, could be faithful to the true momentary looks of the world. The writer, however, whose business was words, seemed to suffer a more distressing upheaval, and was less ready with new techniques. A sense of the desperate rapidity of change, the responsibility of speech in an incomprehensible situation, a feeling of being 'left out', obscure guilt at the inhumanities of a materialistic society: all these may have contributed to his *malaise*. But whatever the 'causes', it was the poet, whose relation to language is always more sensitive and more easily deranged than that of the prose writer, who first showed an extreme reaction. With the symbolists, poetry seemed to take a plunge into a perverse and deliberate obscurity.

The language of poetry is not in the ordinary sense 'communicative'; but it has usually taken for granted the normal power of reference possessed by words and sentences, their power to point fairly unambiguously at items in the world. Precision of reference had been sometimes more, sometimes less, important to the poet; but now suddenly it seemed that the whole referential character of language had become for him a sort of irritant or stumbling block. It was as if the poet began to see the world with a dreadful particularity, as a great ineffable mass of inextricable processes. To lose the discursive ' thingy ' nature of one's vision and yet to feel the necessity of utterance is to experience a breakdown of language—which may be met in either of two extreme ways. The poet may accept and even intensify his sense of the chaotic interpenetration of reality, and attempt to make his language into the perfect expression of this over-rich world. To do this is to weaken the referential character of language by overloading it. On the other hand, the poet may attempt to draw language out of the ineffable flux altogether, and to erect it into a pure and non-referential structure on its own. The former reaction was that of Rimbaud, the latter that of Mallarmé.[2]

Rimbaud seems to seek to achieve a dream-like plenitude wherein language disintegrates through an over-determination of meaning; the thick accumulation of exact and highly sensory imagery produces a rich blending all-enveloping confusion in the mind of the reader. Mallarmé seeks rather to make language perform the impossible feat of simply *being* without referring at all. The reader is held by a pure incantation wherefrom the ordinary senses of the words have been systematically purged. Meaning has been destroyed in the one case by being crowded in, in the other by being charmed out. Characteristic of both poets is the way in which language

[2] I owe the neat model offered by this contrast to Miss Elizabeth Sewell's book *The Structure of Poetry*. See too Jean Paulhan's *Les Fleurs de Tarbes*, which also analyses two extreme tactics in the warfare with language.

appears to them like a metaphysical task, an angel to be wrestled with. Their attention is fixed upon language itself to the point of obsession, and their poems are thing-like, non-communicative, non-transparent to an unprecedented degree; they are independent structures, either outside the world or containing the world. Language loses its character of communicative speech. For both poets, the conclusion is silence : for Rimbaud a real silence, for Mallarmé the self-contradictory ideal silence of a totally pure poetry. Both enterprises have, too, a touch of madness about them. If a certain magical effect can be produced by conjuring with words it is as if some cosmic problem will have been solved, or some cosmic event induced. One is reminded of Kirillov in *The Possessed*, who felt that if *one* free act could be performed the bonds would fall from the whole human race; or else of that imagined splitting of the atom which would dissolve the universe.

Does the world change first and pull language after it, or does a new awareness of language suddenly make us see the world differently? In the various fields where our experience of language was undergoing change, the new thing had the air of being a pure discovery, something which burst unexpectedly upon us, and which was unique, peculiar to the field in question. The philosopher's new self-consciousness about language seemed to him more like an enlightenment than a sickness. ' No one of our recent revolutions in thought is more important than this progressive rediscovery of what we are talking about', wrote I. A. Richards in 1924, in *Principles of Literary Criticism*. It was science, not poetry, however, which revolutionised the philosopher's consciousness of language. The nineteenth-century efflorescence of scientific methods, and the mathematical symbolisms which accompanied them, made the philosopher see the relation of symbols, including words, to reality in a new light. Language was suddenly construed on the model of the scientific definition: the meaning of a sentence being exactly determined by an explanation of the particular sensible observations which would decide its truth. Language was no longer thought of as naming things, even empirical things; it was seen as a way of delimiting, interpreting and predicting sense experience. Metaphysical objects were eliminated and physical objects disintegrated into the appearances, or sensa, which justified statements about them. 'The limits of my language are the limits of my world', Wittgenstein said. With a new sense of power, the philosopher, his attention fixed upon language, began to see words as the determining framework of reality.

With criteria of meaning drawn from the sciences, however, this framework was as yet an extremely restricted one. The meaning of poetry, of religious and theological statements, and of statements in morals and political theory remained problematic. The search, in any case a vain one, for strange objects named by such propositions was gladly discontinued; but it was some time before a patient study was made of their more complex functioning (or 'logic'). Boldly, the language was divided between descriptive (empirical) uses, and emotive uses; and the propositions in question were then said to have 'emotive meaning', to be expressions of feeling without external reference. Even the meaning of poetry became a subject for psychological measurement rather than logical investigation. The immediate result of this move was a loss of confidence in the communicative power of language in these spheres. Language as exact communication seems possible only against the background of a common world, to whose reliable features the uses of words can be related by firm conventions. In the realm of morals and theology, and even political philosophy, a greater sophistication about the function of words seemed to lead to a weakening of that sense of a common world. ' Good ' was no longer thought to name an objective quality, nor ' democracy ' an identifiable form of government; and the alternative appeared to be to regard such words as the recommend-atory cries of beings who, after all, turned out to be a blend of neat reason and neat passion. It was this aspect of the enlightenment, obscurely grasped by lay critics, which occasioned the intermittent storming against ' logical positivism ' as a breeder of cynicism and under-miner of belief in the young. The possibility of honest affirmation seemed to have been taken away. On the other side, however, of this counsel of ' despair ' lay a more patient and self-aware return to the complexities of ' human life '. Gradually the philosopher came to see language not as a structural mirror, or even as a categori-cal frame, of experience of the sensible world, but as one human activity among others. Language and the world no longer stood apart; language now fell into focus as a part of the world, and with this came a readiness to study, on their own merits, the complex ways in which ethical, political, and religious propositions operated.

Yet the powerful fascination of the emotive-descriptive distinction still lingers. It appeals, of course, not purely on account of its dubious philosophical merits. It also gives an intellectual expression and ' justification ' to a real sense of loss : the loss of a world of ideas and values assumed to be common to all thinking beings. The view that political and ethical remarks are simply expressions of emotion might well occur to any critical reader of the daily press. (Just as the view that poetry is sheer disorder might well occur to a reader of Rimbaud!) This weak-ening and obscuring of the sense of moral and political terms is not an accident, however, or even a plot. The smaller, expanding world of the nineteenth century, where the disruptive forces were not only dispossessed and weak, but incoherent, disunited, and speechless, could think itself a single world wherein rational communication on every topic was a possibility. This assumption can no longer be made. The breakdown of the notion of meaning in certain spheres, which might appear to be an achievement of the linguistic philosophers working in isolation, or as the handmaids of science, may also be seen as the consequence of a tragic discovery: the discovery that rational men can have different 'natures' and see the world with a radical difference. So perhaps it was the loss of an actual common background, after all, which occasioned the linguistic sophistication, and not the latter which exposed the former as an illusion. Whatever the reason, we can no longer even imagine that all reflective men have common purposes and common values. In such circumstances, it might be comforting to be able to attribute the resultant difficulties of communication, not to the amendable world or to our corrigible selves, but to an innate peculiarity of the relevant terms. This, in its way, was a surrender to 'the incommunicable', which is said to be 'the source of all violence'.

Poetry was affected first by the linguistic disturbance; prose literature in general, and the novel in particular, were drawn later into the storm area. This was not surprising. The novel, traditionally, is a story, and the telling of a story seems to demand a discursive referential use of language to describe one event after another. The novelist seemed to be, by profession, more deeply rooted in the ordinary world where things were things and words were still their names. Yet, in time, a deep change came about both in the structural technique of the novel and in its page-to-page use of language. The novelist, too, seemed now to turn to literature as to a metaphysical task whereon the sense of the universe was at stake. Compare the attitude of Proust to his work with that of Tolstoy or even Conrad. The writings of the two latter show forth, are nourished by, their answers to life's questions; Proust's work *is* his answer to life's questions. The human task has become a literary task, and literature a total enterprise, wherein what is attempted might be called reconciliation by appropriation.

Many obvious factors combined to unnerve the writer: the rapid change of the social and moral world which ʾrmed his subject-matter, war and ideology and new elements of violence and extremity in daily life, the advent of psychoanalysis. And it was within the ranks of literary people that there then developed the most deliberate and savage attack which had yet been made upon language: Surrealism. Surrealism was born after the 1914 war, under the godmotherly influence of Tristan Tzara's Dadaism, a destructive hate movement, anti-social, anti-literary, anarchical. It developed, under the leadership of André Breton, into a curious revolutionary enterprise. Literature had begun to encroach upon life. The Surrealists set to work to reverse the process. They professed themselves indifferent to art and morality; they were animated by a profound hatred of their society, and an abounding belief in the liberating value of an untrammelled exploration of the unconscious. Poetry was a voyage into dream, language itself simply a medium for automatic utterance, a net for trawling in the depths of the mind, and so extending the bounds of the real; an end which could equally well be reached by other means: *collages*, the fabrication of unnerving objects, or the impact of shocking or pointless acts. For what was sought was not the here today, gone tomorrow, value of ' truth ',

but the undiscriminated richness and particularity of
' reality '.

The Surrealists proclaimed themselves followers of
Rimbaud, opponents of Mallarmé. They rejected the
intellectual fight with language, the attempt to outwit it
and withdraw it from life, or to batter the sense out of it;
they were rather for the swooning surrender to words
which would carry them to subterranean caverns of
encrusted opulence. Rimbaud, moreover, was idolized
for another reason; because he had passed through art
into life, because in the end he had rejected speech,
because he had lived his destiny intensely. That *long,
immense et raisonné dérèglement de tous les sens* which
Rimbaud had said to be the poet's task—a discipline
which was to make of him *le grand malade, le grand
criminel, le grand maudit—et le suprême savant*—was
embraced by the Surrealists as a universal programme of
action. This revolutionary activity could not, however,
remain easily upon the plane of personal salvation. The
Surrealists soon found that they were fellow-travellers,
and ready to assimilate the more romantic aspect of
Marxism.[8] The Moroccan war of 1925 even precipitated
many of them into the Party.

The animating spirit of Surrealism, however, did not
bend easily to Party discipline. Much as the Surrealists
professed to despise literature, they still wished to regard
it as a liberating force in its own right, and not as a tool
of opportunist party tactics. Much as they hated bourgeois society, the revolution for which they yearned was
a revolution of the spirit. The question could not long
be delayed : is there such a thing as Surrealist literature?
And though for a long time the official answer was

[8] ' *Transformer le monde* ', a dit Marx, ' *changer la vie* ', a dit
Rimbaud, ces deux mots d'ordre pour nous n'en font qu'un—
Breton.

negative, yet in fact Surrealist writers could not but become absorbed by the literary techniques which their head-on clash with language had suggested to them. The movement gradually disintegrated into two halves, one part moving on towards direct action by way of the Communist Party, the other part slipping back into literature. Language had won that particular battle; but it had been severely mauled in the process.

The impact of Surrealism upon the themes, technique, and language of the novel in France was immediate, and its effect lasting. Meanwhile, and independently, an impressionist technique had made its appearance in England. Confronted with the chaotic process of the modern world, incomprehensible and gathering speed, and if one can find no place in this process for oneself as actor, or for one's language as instrument, one is after all at liberty to stand back and simply record the particulars as they swirl by, making out of them what wistful personal beauty one can. 'Life is a luminous halo, a semi-transparent envelope surrounding us from the beginning of consciousness to the end ', wrote Virginia Woolf. 'Is it not the task of the novelist to convey this varying, this unknown and uncircumscribed spirit, whatever aberration or complexity it may display, with as little mixture of the alien and external as possible?' The flux whose grey undulations afflicted the hero of *La Nausée* with metaphysical torment is rose-coloured in Mrs. Woolf's work, and her characters take to it as to a natural medium. The logical conclusion of this method is reached in the writings of James Joyce, where (Rimbaud's form of the sickness) the referential nature of language almost gives way under the pressure of the flood of undiscriminated 'reality' demanding expression.

When they wearied of automatic writing the Surrealists went back, though with new skills, to firmer literary forms and steadier uses of language. *Finnegans Wake* reached the extremity alone. The novel moved into what has been called its post-impressionist phase.[4] The impressionist painters tried to paint exactly what they saw, with very startling results. The post-impressionists, by dislocating the ' appearances ' ever so slightly, and colouring them with some special mood of their own, produced something even stranger. (The Surrealists had already discovered how little contriving is required to make some everyday object look grotesque, to turn the photograph into a nightmare.) The novelist went beyond the impressionistic ' realism ' of Mrs. Woolf towards a mood of intellectual play, manipulating ideas, spinning fantasies, and experimenting more light-heartedly with language. Cleverness, brilliance, were now the novelist's attributes. The traditional form of the novel was left, on the whole, to writers of lesser talent, who purveyed, in answer to public demand, easy literature of a faintly ideological kind.

This is the situation of language and literature which Sartre is not alone in deploring. An English critic, D. S. Savage,[5] sees it in terms of a moral failure and a crisis of value. ' Art is speech, and speech is ultimately impossible where there is no absolute existential relation to truth.' According to Savage, the novelists he studies deny this relation, in their various ways, and so move towards ' the impossibility of speech '. Of Huxley's early phase (the key to his later phase) Savage writes : ' Unaware that meaning and purpose do not reside as objective facts in the world of things but are interior realities

---

[4] I owe this extension of the comparison with painting to Professor Bullough. I am not sure if I am making exactly the same use of it.

[5] *The Withered Branch*, a study of Hemingway, Forster, Woolf, Margiad Evans, Huxley and Joyce. See especially Savage's remarks on Joyce's ' magical ' use of language.

which wait for their realisation upon interior dynamic movement, oblivious to the truth that personality is not a substance with which we are endowed by nature, but an inward integration which may be achieved only by the decisive choice of oneself, he arbitrarily attributes his own purposelessness to the universe as a whole' (p. 137). And in discussing Joyce : 'Language is not isolate, is not magical. It is the vehicle of communication, and is related intrinsically to meaning, and through meaning to truth—which is a transcendent value. Language is healthy when it is related directly to meaning, and it can be so related only when the mind itself aspires vertically to truth as an absolute centre' (p. 193).

That meaning and purpose do not reside as objective facts in the world of things was something of which, in fact, people were becoming obscurely conscious. ('In the world everything is as it is and happens as it does happen. *In* it there is no value.' Wittgenstein : *Tractatus* 6.41.) There were a variety of reactions, however, to this breaking of the social and moral fabric. When purposes and values are knit comfortably into the great and small practical activities of life, thought and emotion move together. When this is no longer so, when action involves choosing between worlds, not moving in a world, loving and valuing, which were once the rhythm of our lives, become problems. Emotions which were the aura of what we treasured, when what we treasured was what we unreflectively did, now glow feverishly like distant *feux follets*, or have the imminent glare of a volcanic threat. The attempt to go on making a total sense of the social and political world, as well as acting in it, demanded a new conception of value which connected it with the character and affirmation of the agent.

Those who were deeply concerned with practice on this scale and in the kind which demanded such an interpretation, those thinkers who were committed in a political or religious sense, made the search for truth in action the reconciling and central feature of their philosophies. Such were thinkers of a Marxist or existentialist type. Those who were less concerned, for one reason or another, with ideological activity, with reflexion upon the choice between different worlds, were readier to accept the divided scene at its face value and to take a more dualistic view. Phenomena were divided into the real and the unreal; it was the task of thought to express or mirror the real, and in this passive mirroring or spontaneous expression truth consisted; not in the dynamic picking and choosing, discriminating and evaluating of practical life.

The linguistic philosophers (in their early phase) took as real the facts of science and everyday life; they regarded as unreal the world of art, politics and religion, emotion, fantasy and dream. Value, failing to be *in* the world, was a sort of exclamation. Truth was correspondence with fact, was the sensibly verifiable. Interpretation of human conduct was left to behaviouristic psychologists. This was followed by a more sophisticated and self-consciously anti-dualistic phase, wherein language came to be viewed, no longer as the mirror of the world, but as one human activity among others. Yet the dualism which this philosophy opposed was still a crude version of the mind-body dualism : the Cartesian dualism (thinking and extended substance) and not the Kantian dualism (empirical world and creative spirit). In spite of a more patient treatment of the logic of ethical statements the serious study of the latter dualism was left to the ' committed ' philosophies of the continent.

The Surrealists went the other way; they took as real the passions and desires, the destructive rage of emotion that no longer lived with everyday values and purposes, the lurid figures of the unconscious. To the undiscriminated and unevaluated world of sense they preferred the equally undiscriminated and unevaluated world of dream. This was the 'reality' that concerned the writer, and not the ephemeral value of a 'truth' that was thought out in terms of historical action. The Surrealists were not really concerned with working out the details of a practical programme. They never came to terms with the world sufficiently to do so. Their revolution was the perpetual revolution of romanticism, the violent juxtaposition of the hated bourgeois 'everyday life' and the life of desire; a sounding clash rather than a serious struggle.

Characteristic of both the Surrealists and the linguistic philosophers was the readiness to resolve what seemed a harsh and hopeless dualism into a simple and static monism. This could be done by taking one aspect of life as its total and allowing the other aspects to appear simply as peripheral clouds. For both parties, then, mental activity lost its complexity and depth and appeared as a simple unitary operation: the everyday wielding of tool-like symbols, or the unreflective expression of the contents of the consciousness (it was not Professor Ayer but Tristan Tzara who first said: *la pensée se fait dans la bouche*), while the same rather despairing monistic attitude appears in literature as a readiness simply to record the flux of reality, or to become absorbed in sporting with language itself.

Sartre grew up under the shadow of Surrealism. It was probably in connexion with the Surrealist-Communist struggle that he first encountered the problem of the 'liberating' role of literature; can art liberate without being itself committed? Can it be committed without degenerating into propaganda? Sartre also inherits much of the spirit of Surrealism: he shares its 'heroic' and

exhibitionist temper, its fanatic hatred of bourgeois
society, its cherishing of that flame of intense experience
which was to be not exactly hard and gem-like, but
vigorous, lurid and sweeping. Sartre is infected too with
a certain Trotskyist romanticism, the nostalgia for the
perpetual revolution. Yet he wears all these with a
difference. He is more of a rationalistic intellectual than
a poet by nature, and his experience has sobered him
politically. The rich over-abundance of reality, the phan-
tasmagoria of ' disordered ' sensation, seem to the author
of *La Nausée* a horrifying rather than a releasing spectacle, a threat to the possibility of meaning and truth.
The more surprising contents of the consciousness are
to be interpreted as distorted versions of our deep intentions and not as independent symbols, and certainly not
as strays from a subterranean region of supreme value
and power. Sartre fears, not loves, this notion of a
volcanic otherness within the personality.

On the other hand, he is able to see a certain negative
value in the destructive power of Surrealism and the
literature of the breakdown of sense. False certainties
must be seen through before true ones can be framed;
as moral literature destroys itself, metaphysical literature
imposes itself. ' Human life begins on the other side of
despair.' The crude dualistic scepticism of *Principles of
Literary Criticism* and *Language, Truth and Logic*
taught philosophers something essential, effected the
break with the past; they were then able to move on
from seeing language as mirror or exclamation to seeing
it as an activity in the world among other activities in
the world. But the scene of this activity is for the modern
British empiricist an everyday one from which certain
conflicts are excluded. The ' world ' of *The Concept of
Mind* is the world in which people play cricket, cook
cakes, make simple decisions, remember their childhood

and go to the circus, not the world in which they commit sins, fall in love, say prayers or join the Communist Party.

Sartre too wishes to conceive language neither as a vehicle for realistic reporting nor as an expression of the unsorted totality of the unconscious. Literature is not to be a reconciliation through appropriation, it is to be an activity going forward in a world where certain reconciliations are impossible and certain conflicts inevitable. The world in which Sartre sees language as active is the world of ideological battles, where morality is a function of self-conscious political and religious allegiances and not of a simple and unreflective social round. Sartre wants to put language to work in the context of the great questions of faith; here it is not to be either despised or idolised but used. Sartre's observations are recommendations for the proper use of language rather than analyses of its actual use; and this differentiates him from the British linguistic philosophers. Yet he regards himself as nevertheless expressing an important truth about the human condition when he affirms that language is *properly* a medium of communication.

The hero of *La Nausée* saw language and the world as hopelessly divided from each other. 'The word remains on my lips: it refuses to go and rest upon the thing.' Language was an absurd structure of sounds and marks behind which lay an overflowing undiscriminated chaos: the word which pretended to classify the infinitely and unclassifiable existent, the political slogan or social label or moral tag which concealed the formless heaving mass of human consciousness and human history. Roquentin experiences in an intense and total form that vision of the world which makes men despair of language or else sport with it or even attempt to make it into a self-contained system and a stronghold against chaos. Ro-

quentin himself inclines to a ' literary ' solution of his
dilemma. But what he is concerned to appropriate and
stabilise by these means is simply the shape of his own
life. Roquentin is not Sartre, or is perhaps an aspect of
an immature Sartre. Roquentin's political insight is of a
destructive and negative kind. He is aware that words
may conceal or justify violence and disorder; he seems
unaware that despair of words or their too exclusive
cultivation (' pure literature ' as well as ' the incommunicable ') may do so equally. Or rather it is that while he
sees the absurdity of certain attempts to dominate chaos,
he has no real faith in any salvation other than the
tenuous personal one which he envisages at the close.
What is treated in *La Nausée* as a metaphysical discovery is conceived by Sartre elsewhere as a malady
with political causes and political remedies. The problem is to find a middle way (a third force) between the
ossification of language and its descent into the senseless,
between the bad faith of the *salauds* and spiritual chaos,
between (to translate again) an acceptance of totalitarian
standards (capitalist *or* communist) and political cynicism.
Sartre, as we shall see, going beyond the situation of
Roquentin and beyond his solution, wants to connect in
a great equation literature, meaning, truth, and democracy.

IV

INTROSPECTION AND IMPERFECT SYMPATHY

Zola said that the novelist 'must kill the hero'. He must do this because, according to Zola, his job is to show 'the ordinary course of average lives'. Sartre too believes in killing 'the hero', in the sense of a magnified central figure who enjoys the author's exclusive approval; but for different reasons, reasons connected not with the author's subject-matter but with the author's standpoint. He says: 'No more characters; the heroes are freedoms caught in a trap like all of us.' We can readily give a simple sense to this programme. Sartre is not going to portray for us solid figures with vices and virtues painted upon them. He is going to show us people made transparent by an ambiguous radiance. To do this is not to show the world as futile or senseless, since a *part* of the picture is the urgent demand for sense. In other words, Sartre intends to exhibit his people as more or less reflective moral agents in a peculiarly distracted and uncertain context, and to concentrate upon the quality of their doubt or insincerity. What is the technique which is suited to such an intention?

Sartre says that the mode of self-awareness of the modern novelist is the internal monologue. This seems to be exact. The modern novelist is not usually telling us about events as if they were past and remembered; he is presenting them, through the consciousness of his people, as if they were happening now. The reader is poised, with the character presented, upon the brink of a future whose 'openness' the novelist is at pains to make him feel. This method has both its peculiar appropriateness to the present time (we are not now so anxious to regard minds as *things* which can be adequately described from outside, or from a distance), and also its peculiar difficulties. Sartre himself points out some of the difficulties when he says (*L'Etre et le Néant*, p. 416) : ' Character has no distinct existence except as an object of knowledge to other people. Consciousness does not know its own character—except in so far as it may consider itself reflectively from the point of view of another. . . This is why pure introspective description of oneself does not reveal a character : Proust's hero " has " no character which can be grasped directly.' This need not point to more than a technical problem for the novelist : the problem of how to work in a variety of outside views of each person, so that we may obtain an ' objective ' picture.

Another critic, however, while agreeing with Sartre that introspection does not show character, sees this as a reason for keeping the internal monologue method on a short leash, and regards the popularity of the method as a symptom of literary disease. George Lukacs writes (*Studies in European Realism*, p. 8) : ' The psychologists' punctilious probing into the human soul and their transformation of human beings into a chaotic flow of ideas destroy no less surely every possibility of a literary presentation of the completely human personality ', no less surely, that is, than does a crude ' objectivist ' naturalism. It is between these two extremes, of an impoverished black-and-white objectivism (Upton Sinclair) and an isolated aesthetic subjectivism (James Joyce) that Lukacs sees literature in the western world as condemned to move. For want of the inclination and ability to put the ' decisive social determinants ' of character and action into the picture, the western writer, Lukacs says, has made his characters pale and empty or (if his technique is psychological and subjectivist) eccentric or pathological. That is, to put the accusation in the terms used in the previous chapter, Lukacs charges the western writer, who has evidently lost the aspiration to truth (since such an inspiration would require him to come to terms with Marxism) with portraying his characters in a static monistic manner, as denizens of a simple 'factual' world or an equally simple emotional world, rather than as active beings who can only be properly characterised by being shown in reciprocal connexion with the society they inhabit. And he picks on the introspective technique of the modern novelist as a symptom of a neglect of the complexity of what he takes to be the real nature of human personality.

Now there is a sense in which it is obviously inexact to say that introspection does not reveal character. It is true that self-analysis 'breaks up' the firm configuration to which we usually give the name 'character'—and the 'purer' the analysis the harder, perhaps, to name what is revealed in terms of virtues and vices. Yet an 'impure' analysis will give itself away and readily receive a name. Good glass is invisible, inferior glass can be seen as well as seen through. In Constant's novel *Adolphe*, for instance, which is a prolonged self-analysis with only one voice, we confidently pass judgment, from the quality of the analysis itself, upon the bad faith of the narrator. *Adolphe*, of course, is told retrospectively in the mode of 'the remembered', not of the immediate. The same applies however to the analysis which is presented as 'happening now'. To see the person concerned through the eyes of another may help our evaluation of him—but we do not need this if the author has given sufficient colour to the monologue to enable us to 'place' the narrator. (Narration through a non-reflexive consciousness may of course be equally revealing—as when, in *Anna Karenina*, we learn not only the intensity but the quality of Levin's joy from his finding a tiresome meeting delightful, of Anna's misery from her seeing inoffensive people as beastly.)

If, however, the author cuts up the inner landscape too finely, or, from indifference or some other reason, fails to give us the material on which to judge the quality of the monologue, we may cease to be interested in estimating the good faith of the narrator, and may simply turn to enjoying the subtlety and finesse of the author as this displays itself in the various moments of the analysis. I think this is our situation where certain of Virginia Woolf's people are concerned. The person is presented as a series of more or less discrete experiences, connected by tone and colour rather than by any thread of consistent struggle or purpose—and both person and author seem content. This is certainly one way of 'killing the hero'—but it is not the way which Sartre commends. In *La Nausée* Roquentin experiences a disintegrated world, but, unlike the heroine of that other lyric upon the absurdity of everything, *Mrs. Dalloway*, he does so with acute distress; he feels it *ought not* to be so. In *Les Chemins de la Liberté* the story is related entirely through the moment-to-moment consciousness of the characters, and considerable space is devoted to self-analysis on the part of the main persons; but the interest of the story appears to lie in the *demand* for sense, the characters' determination to find a meaning in their lives. Does Sartre, in spite of his use of the introspective technique, really succeed in creating people who are neither 'pale' nor 'pathological'? Sartre has recommended moral concern as a recipe for good writing. We shall wish to see how the vertical aspiration to truth (which I have no doubt Sartre would consider Virginia Woolf to lack) affects his portrayal of his own people, and in what exactly that aspiration consists.

The character of whom we see most, and on whom our interest centres in the first three volumes of *Les Chemins*, is Mathieu. We receive plenty of oblique information about Mathieu through Ivich's tart comments, Boris's admiration, Daniel's contempt. What do we learn, however, from Mathieu himself, whose monologues occupy so many pages? It seems that, as soon as Mathieu begins · to reflect, *tout fout le camp*. In *Le Sursis*, for instance, when he pauses on the Pont Neuf and contemplates suicide, his reflexions fall apart into a dry senselessness. 'He was alone upon the bridge, alone in the world, and no one could tell him what to do. "I am free *for nothing*", he thought with lassitude ' (p. 286). This is typical of Mathieu's reflexions. At the crises in his life, it is the same note of emptiness and weariness which is struck always. At the close of *L'Age de Raison*, after his break with Marcelle : ' He felt nothing except an anger without an object and behind him the act, naked, smooth, incomprehensible : he had stolen, he had abandoned Marcelle when she was pregnant, *for nothing* ' (p. 288).

This effect of a void at the centre is of course perfectly deliberate. Nor is the random air of this 'freedom of indifference' in itself unconvincing. When Mathieu starts to say ' I love you ' to Marcelle, and says ' I don't love you ', when he tells Pinette resistance is pointless and then reaches for his gun : this is indeed how we behave. In a way too, one might say, it is ' only because ' Myshkin fails to reach the door in time, after the scene between the two women, that he stays with Nastasya and does not wed Aglaia (in *The Idiot*). It is ' only because ' Varenka makes an inopportune remark about mushrooms that Sergei Ivanovich fails to propose to her (in

Anna Karenina). Yet these latter cases affect us differently; they lose their air of total randomness because of the pressure upon them of the whole work of which they are a part.

The danger is that, if a character is presented with an excess of lucidity and transparency, a sense of futility may overcome the reader as well. What is typical of Mathieu is not only his ' anguish ' and ' lack of reasons ' for doing A rather than B—it is his chill self-consciousness about the whole affair. We might compare Sartre's descriptions of Mathieu's choices with the description in *Daniel Deronda* of Gwendolen's decision to marry Grandcourt. The anguish and the ' bad faith ' of the heroine are presented in a mixture of external detail and introspective description : the urgent ' picture book ' recollections, the warm sense of a possible escape, the ' yes ' which she speaks as if in a court of justice.[1] Gwendolen's predicament moves us in a way in which none of Mathieu's manages to do—and a part of the reason for this is the extreme transparency of Mathieu's consciousness. Now Sartre might well answer that to present the matter thus was exactly his purpose. Yet his position as a philosopher has set him a difficult task as a novelist : that of maintaining our interest and our sense of reality in spite of the drying and emptying effect of the perpetual analysis. In their private self-communings Sartre's people do seem in danger of losing our concern either because of their abstraction (Mathieu might indeed be called a ' pale ' character) or else because of their abnormality (Daniel is certainly a 'pathological' character). We cannot here discover any clear answer to the question :

[1] That ' yes ' hits off with beautiful accuracy the kind of bad faith which Sartre too attempts to characterise in *L'Etre et le Néant* by his example of the girl who leaves her hand inert and ' unnoticed ' in the grasp of her admirer (p.95). See also F. R. Leavis's analysis of the *Deronda* passage in *The Great Tradition*.

what does Sartre himself really value? By the magnetic power of what ' truth ' is he led into ' seriousness '? So let us now consider the relation of Sartre's people with each other.

The lesson of *L'Etre et le Néant* would seem to be that personal relations are usually warfare, and at best represent a precarious equilibrium, buttressed as often as not by bad faith. We find nothing in the novels which openly contradicts this view. It is not only that the relationships portrayed in *Les Chemins* are all instances of hopelessly imperfect sympathies—Mathieu and Ivich, Mathieu and Odette, Mathieu and Daniel, Mathieu and Brunet, Mathieu and Marcelle, Gomez and Sarah, Boris and Lola. This in itself is nothing to complain of. Indeed it is in Sartre's ruthless portrayal of the failure of sympathy that we often most feel his penetration and his honesty. What does deserve comment is that Sartre acquiesces in the lack of sympathy in a way which suggests that his interest is elsewhere. He is looking *beyond* the relationship; what he values is not the possibility which this enfolds but something else. One feels this particularly perhaps in the treatment of Marcelle, who is dealt with hardly not only by Mathieu but by her author. Sartre is not really very interested in the predicament of Marcelle, except from the technical point of view of its effect upon Mathieu. Similarly we feel a touch of hardness in the portrayal of Boris's relations with Lola. We are not moved by Lola's situation— whereas we are pierced to the heart by the somewhat similar situation of Ellénore in *Adolphe*. And a part of the reason is that Lola's author does not care very much either; he *accepts* the position. It is not *here* that he has entered absorbingly into his work.

The tragic and magnetic unattainability of the loved other is not presented; and neither is the terribly concrete presence of the hated other shown to us with the force which one might have expected from the author of *L'Etre et le Néant*. This, on second thoughts, is not surprising either. If we are to be either touched or terrified there must be that concrete realisation of what George Eliot called ' an equivalent centre of self from which the shadows fall with a difference '—and this I have suggested Sartre does not give us in the novels. The grasp which his characters have of each other seems flimsy if we compare it with the joyful and terrible apprehension of each other of, for instance, Anna Karenina and Vronsky—or with the relations of Dorothea and Casaubon in *Middlemarch*, that brilliant study of being-for-others. In one place only do we feel that Sartre has entered deeply into the encounter which he portrays, and that is in the friendship between Brunet and Schneider. Only here, and with a momentary intensity verging on the sentimental, is there the flicker of a real ' I— Thou '. One may suspect that some thwarted political passion, connected perhaps with a disappointed love-hate of the Communist Party, lies behind the semi-sexual relation between these two characters. In any case, it is only a flicker; what we are left with is the *meaning*, in terms of the intellectual concerns which rule *Les Chemins*, of the symbolically named and slain Vicarios.

Sartre has commended moral seriousness in the writer. He would agree that the emphasis and configuration of a novel are decided by what the author really values. We have seen that Sartre attaches no value to the intellectual's lonely meditations, nor does he seem to attach much value to the muddled and frustrated efforts of human beings to understand each other. It remains possible that value lies in ' social relations '—in something to do with politics. Here we seem to be closer to the mark. It is certainly clear that the central theme of

Les Chemins is communism. Yet how is this treated? Its presentation to us in Brunet's first phrase is very largely criticism. We acquire a respect for Brunet but not for his ideas. Nor is there any other ' political ' character in the book (certainly not Gomez) whom we are encouraged to regard as on the way to salvation. What is it then that Sartre considers valuable, what is the ' truth ' to which he aspires, and which will give us the key to *Les Chemins de la Liberté*?

V

VALUE AND THE DESIRE TO BE GOD

The answer is of course given in the title : what is valuable
is freedom. But before we can see exactly what this
means we must turn to a brief consideration of Sartre's
philosophy. Sartre is a traditional Cartesian philosopher
in that an analysis of ' consciousness ' is the central
point of his philosophy. This analysis is presented in
L'Etre et le Néant and also, more picturesquely, in *La
Nausée*. Sartre is also Cartesian in his insistence on ' the
supremacy of the *cogito* '; that is, he relies finally upon
the direct deliverance of a consciousness wherein there
can *be* no more than what *appears*. But Sartre is un-
Cartesian in that he does not want to conceive consciousness as a single unitary process of intellection or awareness which is radically separated from physical activity.
On the other hand, he is not prepared to go as far as
certain British empiricists in the direction of identifying
mind or intelligence with its observable concomitants.
His interests are psychological rather than semantic. He
is concerned with the actual varying quality of our
awareness of things and people, rather than with the
question of how, in spite of these variations, we manage
to communicate determinate meanings; he is concerned
with a study of the phenomena of awareness, and not
with the delineation of concepts.

Sartre pictures consciousness by means of two contrasts.
The first is the contrast between the flickering, unstable,
semi-transparent moment-to-moment ' being ' of the consciousness, the shifting way in which it conceives objects
and itself—and the solid, opaque, inert ' in-themselves-

ness' of *things* which simply are what they are. The consciousness, however, is not constantly in a state of translucent or empty self-awareness (we are not always reflecting); usually we are unreflectively engaged in grasping the world as a reality which is coloured by our emotions or intentions. Alternatively, we may be aware of ourselves, not as transparent to our own reflective gaze, but as solidified and judged by the gaze of another. In these ways the consciousness moves from a state of open self-awareness towards a more opaque and thing-like condition; only since the consciousness is not a thing, but however absorbed or fascinated retains a certain self-awareness, or flexibility, or tendency to flicker, it is more appropriate to picture it as a gluey or paste-like substance which may become more or less solidified—and which retains something of its heavy inert sticky nature even in reflective moments. (Introspection is not the focusing of a beam upon something determinate.) 'Glueyness' (*le visqueux*) is for Sartre the image of consciousness; and fascinates us for *that* reason. It is in terms of a solidification, or closing of the texture, that Sartre pictures insincerity or bad faith (*mauvaise foi*): the more or less conscious refusal to reflect, the immersion in the unreflectively coloured awareness of the world, the persistence in an emotional judgment, or the willingness to inhabit cosily some other person's estimate of oneself. It is in terms of a dispersion of this gluey inertness that Sartre pictures freedom; 'freedom' is the mobility of the consciousness, that is our ability to reflect, to dispel an emotional condition, to withdraw from absorption in the world, to set things at a distance.

The other contrast which Sartre uses is that between the flickery discontinuous instability of consciousness (we are moody, lacking in concentration, the 'depth' or 'richness' of our apprehension of our surroundings varies, we cannot hold an object steady for long in our attention, however intense or delighted) and a condition of perfect stability and completion towards which it aspires. This notion of the consciousness as an emptiness poised between two totalities we have already met with in *La Nausée* : as soon as Roquentin has ' seen through ' the thin categories of words, and classes, and social labels, he feels himself immersed in the ' glue ' of nameless ' thinginess ', and his own thoughts seem as shapeless as the rest; yet he still aspires to the realm of circles and melodies. This aspiration Sartre describes in *L'Etre et le Néant* in these terms when he speaks of suffering. ' We suffer, and we suffer from not suffering enough. The suffering of which we *speak* is never quite the same as that which we feel. What we call " true " or " real " or " proper " suffering, suffering which moves us, is what we read on the faces of others, or better still in portraits, on the face of a statue, on a tragic mask. That is suffering which has *being* ' (p. 135). The translucence of our own suffering seems to spoil its depth. It is a suffering which we have to ' make '—and so we feel it to be a sort of sham. ' It speaks incessantly because it is insufficient, but its ideal is silence. The silence of the statue, of the stricken man who bows his head and covers his face without a word ' (p. 136). We wish our experience to become full, steady, and complete, without losing its self-aware transparency : the expressive immobility of the statue, the timeless motion of the melody, are images of this steadiness. Consciousness is *rupture*, it is able to spring out of unreflective thing-like conditions—but it is also *projet*, it aspires towards a wholeness which forever haunts its partial state.

Sartre then goes on (in the passages that follow those quoted above) rather unexpectedly to say this : we are

now able to determine more precisely what the *being* of
the self is—it is value (*la valeur*). Value *is* something
but it is not some thing. It has the double character of
being unconditionally and yet of not being. It is not to
be identified with any actual real quality or state of
affairs; if it is, ' the contingency of being kills the value '.
This much is familiar ground : compare G. E. Moore's
insistence that value is ' non-natural '; Wittgenstein's :
' it must lie outside all happening and being so. For all
happening and being so is accidental ' (*Tractatus* 6.41).
What is harder to understand is that Sartre seems to be
identifying value with that stable lived totality for which
the consciousness is nostalgic. ' The supreme value
towards which consciousness, by its very nature, is constantly transcending itself is the absolute being of the self,
with its qualities of identity, purity, permanence ' (p.
137).

The sense of this appears to be that to value something
is to seek through it to achieve a certain stabilising of
one's own being. No absorption in contingent things can
offer this stability nor can it be found in the shiftings of
a reflective self-consciousness. That which is sought
(valued) is the firmness of thing-like being (*être-en-soi*),
combined with the transparency of consciousness (*être-
pour-soi*) : a state of complete lucidity and complete
changelessness. But this combination is patently unattainable. The self which is excluded by the opaque absurdity
of matter on one side, falls short on the other of this
magnetic totality, which is unattainable because it is
self-contradictory. Such a condition, that of being *en-
soi-pour-soi*, Sartre later says (p.653) is the condition of
being God : it is not a possible human condition. A
sense of value then is a sense of lack, the lack of a certain
completeness; and the reflective consciousness which

reveals to us this lack (under the eye of which what we
are shrivels, as it were, to nothing) is properly called a
moral consciousness.

'Man is the being who aspires to be God', Sartre
writes (p. 653), and at the close of *L'Etre et le Néant*
he embroiders rhetorically upon this theme. The passion
of man is the opposite of that of Christ. Man is to lose
himself as a man in order that God shall be born; that
is, man naturally aspires away from his unsatisfying
human condition towards a state of conscious completeness. But since the idea of God is a contradiction the
loss is vain. *L'homme est une passion inutile.* To understand this is to rid ourselves of the bad faith of the *esprit
de sérieux.* If we imagine that 'the valuable' is a property of the world, or that our tasks are 'written in the
sky' we are doomed to failure and despair. From this
point of view, *revient-il au même de s'enivrer solitaire-
ment ou de conduire les peuples* (it's all the same whether
we get drunk by ourselves or lead the people) (p. 721).
If all human activity is simply one form or another of a
fruitless attempt to be *ens causa sui* then it matters very
little which form we adopt.

Sartre hesitates, however, to end his book unambiguously upon this note of stoical defiance. He has described
to us how we free ourselves from unreflective sluggishness,
aspire through the medium of our various human activities towards a secure condition of pure identity—and,
inevitably, fail and fall back perhaps into a state of self-
deception, masking our essential finitude by an unreflective identification of the valuable with some contingent
thing. But what if we realise our error? What if we
realise that value is a function of the movement or
yearning of our consciousness? What if we trace everywhere, as Sartre does, the same pattern of frustrated
endeavour? Is man condemned to the same fruitless

pursuit, even in his very realisation of its fruitlessness? Is the discovery that all activity is the vain attempt to be God itself a form of this activity? Or can freedom, by its very transparency, put an end to 'the reign of value'? Can the self-aware unillusioned consciousness take itself as a value, or must the valuable be always the transcendent something by which it is haunted? These interesting questions, Sartre tells us, will be answered 'in our next'. This work (a work on ethics) did not appear. But Sartre gives, as we shall see, what is in effect an answer to his own questions in his pronouncements on literature and politics.

METAPHYSICAL THEORY AND
POLITICAL PRACTICE

It seemed from *L'Etre et le Néant* that what Sartre meant by 'freedom' was the reflective, imaginative power of the mind, its mobility, its negating of the 'given', its capacity to rise out of muddy unreflective states, its tendency to return to an awareness of itself. For this sense of freedom, needless to say, stone walls make no prison; we are potentially free so long as we are conscious. It seemed, too, that what Sartre meant by 'value' was a notion of completeness which haunted the free consciousness and towards which it vainly aspired. This aspiration would, of course, take the form of some particular human project (getting drunk by oneself or leading the people). What Sartre is trying to analyse for us is the structure of all human consciousness and human endeavour. It might very appropriately take the form of the creation or enjoyment of a work of art.

The reflective consciousness thought of as 'imagining' still runs the danger of falling into bad faith, that is of losing its tense mobility and degenerating into a 'gluey' unreflective condition. Imagination may be seen as a 'break' with the given world, which then continues into an imaginative state which has more or less of a self-prolonging inertia. This inertia may lead to a further *empâtement* or 'fall' of the consciousness into unreflective sluggishness. This move might correspond, presumably, to a change from tense creative imagining to vague day-dreaming. Sartre describes imagination as a *spontanéité envoûtée*. Aesthetic enjoyment then seems readily to connect with both the mobile or 'free' aspect of the consciousness and with its perilous aspiration towards the 'valuable'.

The goal of art, Sartre writes in *What is Literature?* (p. 41) is 'to recover this world by giving it to be seen as it is, but as if it had its source in human freedom'. The work of art, depending as it does upon the reader or spectator for its existence, is an appeal, a demand. The reader too must be the creator of the novel; his continuing to read it 'properly', that is to enter into it seriously, to 'lend' it his emotions and so on, involves him in a sustained act of faith in the work itself. The imagination must be enchanted, but, I think Sartre would agree, not too enchanted. An excessive detachment or suspicion will fail to create the work at all; an excessive self-forgetfulness will break down its objective contours and blend it with private fantasy and dream. In the latter case novel-reading becomes a drug. (It is characteristic of the art of the cinema to encourage, by its very form, this extreme of self-forgetting.) Our *delight* in a work of art is our sense of the imaginative activity involved in creating it and maintaining it, as it were, just at the right distance from ourselves. The novel is, in this sense, 'a task set to freedom'. The seeing of the world as if it originated in human freedom does not mean of course any remoulding of it closer to the heart's desire, for we still see it 'as it is'. But in the formal 'necessity' of the artist's vision, and of ours when we see with his eyes, we get a taste of the Godlike power of intellectual intuition. Aesthetic joy involves 'an *image-making* consciousness of the world in its totality both as being and having to be' (*What is Literature?* p. 43). Thus far what Sartre is saying would seem to be a restatement in his own terminology of a piece of traditional post-Kantian aesthetics. Aesthetic enjoyment is an active reflective awareness which seeks to apprehend through the material presented to it some autonomous totality of experience in whose internally related completeness it may achieve the repose of a perfect equilibrium. This movement, which so clearly follows the form which Sartre attributes to all human striving, cannot however (if we are to credit *L'Etre et le Néant*) afford any lasting satisfaction.

'The real is never beautiful', Sartre wrote in *L'Imaginaire* (p. 254). 'Beauty is a value which can apply only to the imaginary and whose essential structure involves the nullification (*néantisation*) of the world. This is why it is foolish to confuse ethics and aesthetics. The values of the Good presuppose being-in-the-world, they are concerned with behaviour in real contexts and are subject from the start to the essential absurdity of existence.' Yet it would seem that in *What is Literature?* what Sartre is finally concerned with is precisely behaviour in real contexts. He is connecting the value of prose literature with its proper function and appearing to deduce the latter from the metaphysical view of consciousness outlined above. Since describing or naming is revelation, the writer can never be a neutral observer. Is there perhaps something in the nature of his calling which indicates *how* he should describe the world? Sartre thinks that there is. Since the novel is an appeal to freedom, since it presupposes as reader a free man, there would be a sort of contradiction involved in using the novel to advocate enslavement. 'The writer, a free man addressing free men, has only one subject—freedom.'

The good novelist then, the one who is not the dupe of his subject-matter, who has transformed his emotions into free emotions, cannot but in the process of this discipline have learnt the importance and value of freedom. For him, 'to show the world is to disclose it in the perspectives of a possible change'. His reader, moreover, in responding to the writer's demand, 'strips himself in some way of his empirical personality and escapes from his resentments, his fears, and his lusts in order to put himself at the peak of his freedom. This freedom takes the literary work and, through it, mankind, for absolute ends' (p. 200). In this way the reader joins himself to a sort of Kingdom of Ends wherein the *good wills* of all his fellow readers are united. In his response to the writer he is exercising, with a peculiar purity, a kind of respect for the free play of human personality, he is rising to an ability to respond unselfishly to the vision of the writer which in so far as it is a ' free ' vision, not ruled by private passion or fantasy, both constitutes good art *and* commands an absolute moral respect.

This respect for freedom, this taking of mankind as an absolute end, cannot however remain within the bounds demanded for the appreciation of a work of literature. This fire, once kindled, will spread itself. The good will asks to be historicised. Who wills the Kingdom of Ends is not far from willing the open society. Both writer and reader cannot consistently enjoy the free creative activity of the making and appreciating of literature, and yet consent that this shall take place in a society which is in other respects ruled by blind passion, prejudice or other arbitrary confinements of the spirit. It is an inevitable part of the task of the novelist, not only to exemplify this liberating creativity of art, but (since he cannot, from the nature of his subject-matter, avoid commenting on society) to advocate a community of free beings. This he will in fact do, with more or less self-consciousness, if he is writing well. A part of his public consumes its good will in personal relationships, while another part is simply concerned to better its material lot. The novelist will teach to both the connexion between the pure liberating pleasures of the spirit, and the protection and promotion of a certain disposition of society. (See *What is Literature?* pp. 204-205.)

This is a rather breath-taking argument. That the novel comments on society is on the whole true. It is also easy to see why prose literature in general and the novel in particular are most suited to 'commitment' (*engagement*), the transforming of the appeal to 'freedom' which is made by all art into a more specific kind of social recommendation. What is surprising, particularly after the introduction to Sartre's thought afforded by *L'Etre et le Néant*, is this. By 'value', Sartre appeared to mean a vain aspiration towards a state of personal equilibrium, of which art might indeed be one form, while solitary inebriation might be another. From the point of view of *L'Etre et le Néant*, *any* art ('good' or 'bad') might give form to this aspiration. In *La Nausée* Roquentin receives the idea of the perfection he craves from an indifferent piece of music. In *What is Literature?*, however, a certain discrimination has been made. The writer who has purged himself of narrowing personal lusts and fantasies, who has 'converted his emotions into free emotions', is singled out as having achieved a value which is denied to one who has eschewed this discipline. This purging is clearly regarded by Sartre as being somehow *proper* to the human spirit, morally valuable, and also productive of *good* art. Both the moral and aesthetic value here in question seem to be 'values' in something much closer to the ordinary sense of that word than to the use it receives in *L'Etre et le Néant*; and the 'freedom' which Sartre still speaks of as being the characteristic *élan* of the consciousness is no longer a fruitless drive towards stability which anything might appear to satisfy, but a particular disciplined activity which is contrasted with other less admirable ones.

A clue to the change which has taken place is given by Sartre's use of the term 'Kingdom of Ends'. *L'Etre et le Néant* claimed to be a work of a *descriptive* type. 'Phenomenological ontology' was what Sartre said that it was, and not 'metaphysics'. Sartre expressly denied, that is, that he was offering a metaphysical theory of human nature in that book. The *content* of human endeavour was, from the point of view of *L'Etre et le Néant*, personal and accidental. The model presented was of the form or structure of that endeavour, and it went beyond 'the facts' of human behaviour in a way comparable to that in which the Freudian mythology goes beyond the facts. The concepts of *être-en-soi*, *être-pour-autrui*, and the rest may be thought of as playing a hypothetical explanatory role similar to that played by Freud's egos, ids, and censors: equally illuminating and equally in danger of misleading their author if not carefully handled.

We now find Sartre using the notion of a kingdom of harmonising ends wherein human wills are to be united. That human ends in fact harmonise is clearly empirically false. This notion has no descriptive role. It is apparently being used by Sartre in a way similar to the way it was used by Kant, as a regulative idea. Sartre seems now to be saying that if we make a *proper* exercise of our freedom, which will involve our taking mankind as an absolute end, we shall tend towards a harmony in willing. In Sartre's popular pamphlet *L'Existentialisme est un Humanisme* we find the same notion put forward even more simply and boldly and used as a political weapon. In this work Sartre presents in dramatic and polemical form his view of the 'non-existence' of value prior to action. There is no essence or nature of Man

(in an Aristotelian or any other sense) to act as a given
objective ideal. I create value by my choices—as I
might create a work of art—according to no pre-existing
model. This means, Sartre adds, that I am responsible
for the image of man in general which my behaviour
suggests. ' I am responsible for myself and for everyone,
and I create a certain image of man which I choose;
in choosing myself I choose man.' Further, once it is
clear to me that freedom is the *basis* of all value I cannot
but will freedom, in some concrete manifestation or
other, as a desirable end. (This Sartre frankly offers as
' a moral judgment', p. 82. He hesitates to say though
that I *ought* to will freedom; he says that if I understand
the situation I ' can only ' will it.) ' The ultimate meaning of the actions of men of good faith is the pursuit of
freedom as such. . . I cannot take my own freedom as
an end without also taking the freedom of others as an
end.'

It seems a long way from the heroic solipsism of *L'Etre
et le Néant* to this Kantian argument with its implicit
social conclusions. Sartre now appears to be deducing
from his view of human consciousness that a particular
condition of society is the most natural and proper one
for creatures so framed. Sartre is of course not the first
to deduce political imperatives from the nature of man.
Kant and Rousseau, whom he here closely follows, connected the notion of freedom as the characteristic of
consciousness with the nature of the ideal society. There
is however a certain obscurity, or even lack of frankness,
in the way Sartre has moved on from description to
recommendation. Sartre connects in an equation freedom as a general attribute of consciousness, freedom as
the openness of our response to a work of art, and
freedom in the sense it has acquired in the politics of

contemporary social democracy. He is able to make this explosive juxtaposition with the help of the Kingdom of Ends concept, and by means of a stupefying ambiguity in the use of the word 'freedom'.

'Freedom' in the sense in which Sartre originally defined it is the character of *any* human awareness of anything : its tendency to 'flicker', to shift towards a reflective state; its lack of equilibrium. Sartre speaks of it in *L'Etre et le Néant* as if it were a sort of *scar* in the wholeness of the consciousness; a sort of fault in the universe. It is a *néant*. The second sense of 'freedom' is one which would need to be defined much more closely than Sartre defines it in *What is Literature?*, but which in any case is not the same as the first since it is not a characteristic of *any* consciousness. It seems more like a sort of spiritual discipline; it is a *purging* of the emotions, a setting aside of *selfish* considerations, a respect for the autonomy of another's (the writer's) creative power, which leads on to a respect for the autonomy of all other men (the 'taking of mankind as an absolute end'). To be 'at the peak of one's freedom' is clearly, as Sartre uses the phrase, both difficult and morally admirable. This sense of 'freedom' seems closely allied to the rational will of Kant and Rousseau. That Sartre hesitates between thinking of freedom as a fever and as a discipline is already apparent in the novels if we look more closely. In *La Nausée* freedom is *both* the absurd emptiness or quaking gelatinous texture which Roquentin apprehends in his own consciousness—*and* the reflective power which enables him to see through the pretensions of the *salauds*. It is both the instability of the momentary consciousness and the disciplined avoidance of the settled illusion. And in *Les Chemins*, when Mathieu is thinking about Marcelle, his 'freedom ', which bids him desert her, seems to him ' like a crime, like a grace '—like random blundering, like spiritual liberation.

' Freedom ' in the third sense is that which it is self-contradictory for a writer to traduce, that which I must effectively will for others as well as myself if I am exercising my consciousness as a human being ' properly '. This freedom is an ideal state of society, the willing of which imposes practical commands of an anti-totalitarian nature upon its adherents. In this sense (the sense particularly in which it is used in *L'Existentialisme est un Humanisme*), the word readily picks up the flavour of that vague but powerful *liberté* in the name of which we fought fascism. It becomes a weapon to use against the soul-destroying ossifications of both capitalism and communism. Freedom in the first sense can easily be shown to be the characteristic *par excellence* of human awareness. This sense is connected with sense two by the dual meaning of ' reflexion ' as a destructive reflexive flicker and as a disciplined restraint. Sense two then merges, with the help of the Kingdom of Ends concept, into sense three, and the conclusion is that human nature demands a modified form of socialism.

VII

THE ROMANCE OF RATIONALISM

It is no superficial or perverse dilemma into which this
thinker has got himself. As a European socialist intellectual with an acute sense of the needs of his time Sartre
wishes to affirm the preciousness of the individual and
the possibility of a society which is free and democratic
in the traditional liberal sense of these terms. This
affirmation is his most profound concern and the key to
all his thought. As a philosopher however he finds himself without the materials to construct a system which
will hold and justify these values; Sartre believes neither
in God nor in Nature nor in History. What he *does*
believe in is Reason; and this is what chiefly differentiates
him from the positivist, whose dislike of traditional
speculative metaphysics is equally vehement.

Sartre finds traditional bonds inert and entangling;
what appears to Gabriel Marcel as a rich substantial
connexion with a fruitful and living tissue is for Sartre a
fall into insincerity, inertia and unreason. The undivided
nature which haunts him is not the totality of the perfectly unreflective, but the totality of the perfectly reflective, the spiritual *tabula rasa*. Sartre is a rationalist;
for him the supreme virtue is reflective self-awareness.
Yet this very quality of his respect for Reason sets him
apart too from the rationalism of the Marxist. Sartre
prizes sincerity, the ability to see through shams, both
social shams and the devices of one's own heart. He
prizes Reason in itself, as a manifestation of the spirit,
rather than prizing it as a means to an end. Whereas
the Marxist, who can see the world as a set of practical

problems to which he knows the answer, attends naturally to the activity of solving the problems and not to
the preliminaries of private reflexion. The rationalism
of Sartre is not geared on to the techniques of the modern
world; it is solipsistic and romantic, isolated from the
sphere of real operations. He shares with thinkers such
as Michael Oakeshott and Marcel their distrust of 'the
scientist'. In the argument appended to *L'Existentialisme est un Humanisme* the communist Naville accuses
Sartre of having *un mépris des choses* (contempt for
things); and adds that existentialists 'do not believe in
causality'. The Marxist can be a confident utilitarian
because he has both a clear idea of human good and an
understanding of the mechanism of social cause and
effect. Sartre lacks both. His Reason is not practical
and scientific, but philosophical. His Evil is not human
misery or the social conditions, or even the bad will,
which may produce it, but the unintelligibility of our
finite condition. 'The artist has always had a special
understanding of Evil, which is not the temporary and
remediable isolation of an idea, but the irreducibility of
man and the world of Thought' (*What is Literature?*
p. 86).

What Sartre does understand, the reality which he has
before him and which he so profoundly and brilliantly
characterises in *L'Etre et le Néant*, is the psychology of
the lonely individual. Behind this personage lies neither
the steady pattern of a divine purpose, nor the reliable
constellations of Newtonian physics, nor the dialectical
surge of work and struggle. The universe of *L'Etre et
le Néant* is solipsistic. Other people enter it, one at a
time, as the petrifying gaze of the Medusa, or at best as
the imperfectly understood adversary in the fruitless
conflict of love. What determines the form of this egocentric and nonsocial world are the movements of love

and hate, project and withdrawal, embarrassment and domination, brooding and violence, fascination and awakening, by which the individual 'takes' his life. There is no *reason* why the personage portrayed in *L'Etre et le Néant* should prefer one thing to another or do this rather than that—unless perhaps it were to avoid the *discomfort* of, say, being observed, or pursuing some peculiarly fruitless end. The analyses offered in *L'Etre et le Néant* may increase self-knowledge, lead to a starting point—but not indicate a road. There is indeed a certain value which is implied by these studies which is not the value that is analysed. That is the value of the liberated clairvoyant disillusioned awareness of the truth. This is the 'freedom' of a personal liberation from insincerity and illusion, and might be the virtue of a life devoted to purely private ends.

When we turn to the novels we find the same spectacle of a struggle towards sincerity and reflexion which can bear no practical fruits. 'The reflective consciousness is the moral consciousness', Sartre said, because it is the revealer of incompleteness and so of the vision of ' value', the whole whose shadow defines a lack. Yet the reflective consciousness of Sartre's fictional characters is empty and their reflexion merely denuding. Sartre's individual is neither the socially integrated hero of Marxism nor the full-blooded romantic hero who believes in the reality and importance of his personal struggle. For Sartre the ' I ' is always unreal. The real individual is Ivich, opaque, sinister, unintelligible and irreducibly other; seen always from outside. Real personal communication is the communication Ivich has with Boris, the nature of which remains impenetrably obscure both to Mathieu and to his author. (Ivich and Boris always fall silent when they see Mathieu approaching.) The simple virtues of human intercourse become forms of insincerity. Only

reflexion and freedom are desired as ends and yet these
turn out to be without content. What the aspiring spirit
achieves is an empty babbling; what it desires is complete
stillness. 'Its ideal is silence.' The individual seen from
without is a menace, and seen from within is a void.
Yet there is a further assertion which Sartre is making
in *Les Chemins*; a passionate 'nevertheless'. We find
this in the Schneider episode, brief, obscure and heavily
charged with emotion.

George Lukacs praises Simone de Beauvoir for seeing
that in this age there is only one moral problem : what
to do about Communism. (Her two philosophical essays,
Pyrrhus et Cinéas and *Pour une Morale de l'Ambiguité*
deal largely with problems of political belief and action.)
This is the problem which obsesses Sartre also; and it is
his guilt-stricken obsession with this either/or which seems
to daze his ethical sensibility in other respects and permits
him to treat personal relations at the level of the psychological casebook. Under the pressure of this enormous
choice ordinary moral distinctions lose their interest. In
Simone de Beauvoir's writings the distress receives a
kind of answer. The hero of *Le Sang des Autres* pain-
fully discovers his moral involvement with other people;
his lightest move, his very existence, bruises another, in
love and politics alike. He leaps from simplicity to a
state of metaphysical neurosis where it seems to him
impossible to draw any limit to his responsibility. But
later he discovers that the 'solution' lies in the struggle
for the society of free beings where a mutual respect for
personality, for the claim of each to choose his own way,
shall end our violences to each other or at least render
them innocent.

Sartre is less naïve and less optimistic about the possibility of our ever managing to be 'as free as before'.
The innocence which stands to Simone de Beauvoir as a

serious ideal[1] appears in *Les Chemins* as Mathieu's fleeting vision of the earthly paradise. The romantic answer emerges without social democratic trimmings, and is given in all its crudeness in the climax on the bell tower. Sartre dissociates himself from this piece of gratuitousness, but not with the conviction of one who clearly envisages another way. *Seule la révolte est pure*[2] is something which Sartre feels, but to which he does not deceive himself into imagining he can give the form of a practical programme.

What Sartre does attempt to assert is the absolute value of the person and the moment, the individual in the moment; that all moments are equidistant from eternity. But he has to make this assertion without the support of any background faith, religious or political. Simone de Beauvoir reduces the moral commandments, whether social or personal, to one: respect freedom. Sartre, though he makes a theoretical use of this ideal, does not give it flesh in *Les Chemins*. Here his defence of the moment appears naked and desperate and unavoidably ambivalent. The moment can wear the secretive selfish face of Ivich as well as the tragic face of Schneider. Its autonomy can be that of a non-rational egoistic will. At best it is the lonely unjustified individual who stands before the Grand Inquisitor; the scapegoat Vicarios, uncertain and shadowy, bitter and ineffectual, one of those who is but too conscious of having fallen out of History, and who is aware of this as an inevitable yet crushing moral failure. The value of the person is detected by Sartre, not in any patient study of the complexity of human relations, but simply in his experience

---

[1] Partly perhaps because she belongs to a race whose liberation can still be conceived as a proper task of Reason and one which is within its power. See her book *Le Deuxième Sexe*.

[2] Simone de Beauvoir, *Les Temps Modernes*, XVII, p. 857.

of the pain of defeat and loss. In cool moments the individual is mercilessly analysed; his preciousness is apprehended only in the emotional obscurity of a hopeless mourning. ('No human victory can efface this absolute of suffering.') It is as if only one certainty remained : that human beings are irreducibly valuable, without any notion of why or how they are valuable or how the value can be defended.

'If the Party is right, I am more lonely than a madman; if the Party is wrong . . . the world is done for.' Sartre does not think that the Party is right and does not want to think that the world is done for. His explicit intention is to make more real to us the possibility of a political middle way; to render us more conscious of our freedom to *make* a destiny that is other than the two crushing alternatives which appear to be offered; to emphasise the value of an innocent and vital individualism which is menaced from both sides. Yet as a theoretician of the third way Sartre has nothing more positive to cling to than this last fragment of faith in the preciousness of the human person, stripped at last of its traditional metaphysical ramifications. On the one hand lies the empty reflexion of a reason which has lost faith in its own power to find objective truth, which knows its idea of an unprecarious liberty to be contradictory, and which finds human suffering a scandal and a mystery. On the other lies the dead world of things and conventions, covering up the mute senselessness of the irrational, where the other person is a Medusa and the only escape is in ' going away ' or in ' losing oneself '. (For Roquentin, both social conventions and linguistic conventions are there, like the green surface of the sea, to cheat us.) The empty consciousness flickers like a vain fire between the inert petrifying reality which threatens to engulf it and the impossible totality of a stabilised freedom. There is total freedom or total immersion, empty reflexion or silence.

The deadening civilisations of capitalism and communism are alike rejected and the perfect society where complete stability combines with complete individual awareness, social security with civil liberty, seems less and less possible. So when one is caught between the intolerable and the impossible nothing is justified except a state of rebellion, however vain. When in insuperable practical difficulties a sense of ' all or nothing ' is what *consoles*. Sartre, who rejects the comfort of the appeal to tradition and unreason, seems to take refuge instead in a deliberately unpractical ideal of rationality. The solipsistic psychology of reflexion mirrors what Lukacs (in almost the same words as Oakeshott uses to describe the Marxists) has called the politics of adolescence.[8] According to this critic, Western man is indeed *vis-à-vis de rien*; he desires nothing but freedom, yet freedom is an empty ideal. The general impression of Sartre's work is certainly that of a powerful but abstract model of a hopeless dilemma, coloured by a surreptitious romanticism which embraces the hopelessness.

It is patent that what many readers of Sartre find in his writings is a portrait of themselves. A likeness is always pleasing, even if one is not handsome; and to be told that one's personal despair is a universal human characteristic may be consoling. But this is not to say that what we are offered here is nothing but an irresponsible caricature of a modern mood. Sartre's great negatives are not the negatives of cynicism, but of an obstinate and denuded belief, which clings to certain values even at the expense of seeming to make them empty. The

[8] George Lukacs, *Existentialisme ou Marxisme?*, p. 196.

Marxists revile Sartre because he describes man as a fundamentally non-social, non-historical individual. But what Sartre wishes to assert is precisely that the individual has an absolute importance and is not to be swallowed up in a historical calculation. Sartre's man is depicted in the moment-to-moment flux of his thoughts and moods, where no consistent pattern either of purposeful activity or of social condition can easily be discerned; at this level freedom seems indeed like randomness, the freedom of indifference.

Sartre wishes at all costs to withdraw his man to a point at which he is independent of what seems to him the inhuman determinism of the modern world, the realm of the economist and the sociologist—even if it means depicting him as an empty shell. 'We stand for an ethics and art of the finite', Sartre wrote in *What is Literature?* Yet because Sartre cannot rid himself of the absolute aspiration, the desire for certainty and completion which he presents as an eternal characteristic of man, he wishes nevertheless to create a *total* picture of the broken totality, to describe man's limit from a point beyond that limit. And because he finds nothing that he values in either of the alternative civilisations which confront him he makes his picture as empty and abstract as possible. He asserts simply the absolute nature of the individual even if he is without hope and the sacredness of reason even if it is fruitless.

Sartre's play on the word ' freedom ' may be a flagrant case of ' persuasive definition '; but it is also a symptom of a dilemma in which we are all involved. For many reasons, the chief of which is that science has altered our societies and our key concepts with a dreadful speed, it seems now impossible for us either to live unreflectively or to express a view of what we are in any systematic terms which will satisfy the mind. We can no longer formulate a general truth about ourselves which shall encompass us like a house. The only satisfied rationalists today are blinkered scientists or Marxists. But what we hold in common, whatever our solution, is a sense of a broken totality, a divided being. What we accuse each other of is 'metaphysical dualism'. All modern philosophies are philosophies of the third way.

VIII

PICTURING CONSCIOUSNESS

I have considered Sartre's theories in the light of his practical interests. Now I shall look at them simply as 'philosophy' in the traditional sense. To consider them only in the latter way would be misleading; Sartre's political passions mark all his work and are responsible for inconsistencies which would be incomprehensible to someone viewing him as an academic philosopher. But to consider his work too exclusively in a political light is to risk underestimating his qualities as a thinker. He is at his most original (philosophically) when he is at his least persuasive.

If we think naïvely about sense perception we can imagine it as the taking of a series of snapshots. Such a thought lies behind the 'magic lantern' view of consciousness held by Locke,[1] Berkeley and Hume. Percepts are one kind of snap, and emotions, or thoughts of absent things, are other kinds. Kant and Hegel upset this notion by introducing problems about the *meaning* of the ideas, and about how the observer might be shaping or altering them. Subject and object sprang together. Later idealists such as Husserl still tried to speak of objects of consciousness as if they were identifiable pictures passing before the mind; and Freud occasionally uses this sort of language too. The metaphysical problems suggested by such a view have been under consideration for a long time; more recently an empirical objection was framed. We do not in fact experience any such thing. Sartre, with his Cartesian starting point, brooding

[1] See for instance Locke's *Essay* II, xiv, 9.

over the moment-to-moment deliverances of consciousness, is impressed by this. *La Nausée* is at pains to portray the indeterminate and nebulous character of many of our 'states of consciousness'. For this, the magic lantern is not a good image. Sartre is not an adherent, either, of the cognate view of consciousness as what Professor Ryle has called 'the ghost in the machine'. As he does not think of awareness as a clear rational stream of ideas, he does not think of it as a stream in parallel to our actions.

What are the memorable examples used in *L'Etre et le Néant*? The gambler whose resolutions melt near the gaming table, the woman who prolongs her indecision by leaving her hand inertly in the grasp of her admirer, the watcher at the keyhole who suddenly realises that he himself is watched, the stroller in the park whose solitary scene is transformed by the arrival of another observer. Sartre remains interested in the deliverances of consciousness because of the role which our attempted conceptualisings of ourselves play in relation to our conduct; and the feature of our awareness which for Ryle marks the inner world as beyond salvage is for Sartre its most important feature. Consciousness is 'troubled'; we are not able to contemplate our states of consciousness, they are not thing-like. Conscious belief turns into unbelief,[2] our 'characteristics' exist for other people, but seem to vanish before our own gaze. Sartre is interested in man not so much as a 'rational' being but as a 'reflective' being : self-picturing, self-deceiving, and acutely aware of the regard of others.

How does Sartre set about describing our consciousness, or our 'being'? We have already encountered the recurrent image, incarnated particularly in Roquentin

---

[2] Sartre was of course not the first to be struck by these problems. Consider the character of Stavrogin in *The Possessed*.

and Daniel, of the consciousness (*pour-soi*) as a sort of
uneasy void (*néant*) lying between a state of unreflective
solidification (*en-soi*) and an ideal but impossible condition of fully reflective self-contemplative stability (*en-
soi-pour-soi*). I shall now try to give a clearer philosophical sense to this image. We may if we please picture
the world ' realistically' as an assembly of things with
stable and determinate characteristics; and even the
nebulous things therein offer themselves as capable of
being named and defined. This is not a complete picture,
however, since we have still omitted the observer. As
soon as we attend to him, we realise not only that his
awareness of the things which he takes to be stable and
determinate is not itself stable and determinate, and that
he is also aware of ' things', such as his own emotions,
which do not at all lend themselves to being observed
and specified; we also realise that, after all, the solid
things of the world do not have their qualities unambiguously written upon them. It is the observer who draws
lines and affixes labels. An acute realisation of this is
one way of beginning philosophy. It also puts one in
immediate danger of going too far in the other direction.
(The move from realism to idealism can be instantaneous : consider Berkeley.)

Sartre says that he wishes to describe consciousness
' not as the totality of the human world but as its instantaneous kernel' (*L'Etre et le Néant*, p. 111). He wishes
to retain the truth which the idealists discovered when
they thought of the observer as the source of meaning;
and yet not to fall into their error of transforming the
world into a set of meanings which are simply the cor-
relatives of acts of attention. Their original mistake,
Sartre holds, is to think of reflective awareness as a
kind of knowledge, and then to model all consciousness
upon reflective consciousness. Sartre wishes to show

'what the world is like' by giving an account of 'how we see the world', which does not reduce our 'self-presence' to a static self-reflexion, but portrays both the elusive nature of momentary awareness and the dramatic nature of our more extended views of ourselves. In doing so he is anxious to avoid equally the error (which he attributes to Heidegger) of describing the world in terms of modes of experience from which the element of reflective self-awareness is omitted and the error (which he would no doubt attribute to Ryle) of skirting behaviourism by neglecting the self-conceptualising and self-dramatising nature of the human mind.

The Marxists were not the only ones to turn Hegel's 'rational' dialectic into a 'real' dialectic. Kierkegaard did the same, but in a very different way. Developments which Hegel conceived as the rational evolving of one idea from another, a process having the objectivity and inevitability of a deduction, Kierkegaard pictured as real spiritual (or psychological) movements of a personality from one phase (mood, or type of outlook) to another. These movements were subjective, reversible, and by no means inevitable. Sartre too thinks of consciousness as 'dialectical', but the dialectic consists of actual shifts of awareness from one condition to another. Only whereas Kierkegaard's 'stages' correspond to types of character or at least deep psychological phases in which a person might persist for long, Sartre is including also in his description the shifts which a consciousness may undergo from one moment to the next. These are real changes, experienced by the individual; not metaphysical motions, transcendentally deduced, which 'must be presumed' to have taken place.

The consciousness, according to Sartre, has three modes: unreflective awareness, reflexion, and being for others. The consciousness itself 'is' nothing; it is a slope on which I cannot stay. I cannot examine and hold my awareness as I can examine and hold that which I am aware of. The consciousness in all its modes has a quality of inertia : that tendency to remain *empâtée* or *envoûtée* of which mention has been made before. We do not, at every moment, spring back into a reflective condition and explicitly notice how it is that we are 'taking' our surroundings. At 'ordinary' times the possibility of reflecting simply does not occur to us—at other times (in certain emotional conditions for instance) it is envisaged but rejected.

In an unreflective condition we are implicitly aware of ourselves. This implicit awareness Sartre calls *conscience (de) soi*, and sometimes he calls it 'the pre-reflective cogito'. It is that on which the reflective awareness may at any moment turn back. It is the condition which classical philosophy has neglected in favour of the reflective *cogito* (or the 'simple idea', which represents the same starting point). What we are explicitly aware of at such times however is not ourselves being aware, nor even a particular determinate mental datum as such—but the world provoking or inviting us in some particular way or charged with some particular properties.

This view of the world we may at any moment call into question. Such reflexion will usually take the form of a reshuffling of the pattern 'out in the world', without any very clear awareness of our own activities of ordering and estimating. Sometimes however the doubt will bite us in such a way as to make us very much aware of ourselves as the source of a certain way of seeing things—in a case of moral doubt, for instance (' am I distorting this situation?') or amid the uneasiness induced by the sudden presence of an observer. Attention is now fixed, not on the world of tasks and provo-

cations, but upon the mind which permits itself to be
provoked and apprenticed. Yet such a reflexion is not
a steady contemplation of psychic data, since psychic data
cannot be contemplated. Psychologists have only thought
they could be because they seemed to be able to characterise state of mind in the recent past. (Compare Ryle
again here, who agrees that introspection is really retro-
spection—*The Concept of Mind*, p. 166.) We are
tempted, however, to create for ourselves at this point a
spurious object : our character or nature, which we may
imagine to be causally related to our conduct. This is
what Sartre calls *la réflexion complice*, or bad faith.
The 'reason' in whose power of purifying reflexion he
believes is not contemplative, is not a form of knowledge.
From the more satisfying activities of *la réflexion çom-
plice* arise not only my uncritical pictures of the inner
forces that rule me, but also, Sartre would say (and
again Ryle would agree, though he would put it differently), most of contemporary psychology, and much of
traditional philosophy. The determination to regard
consciousness itself as a source of knowledge, illuminating
its own acts, leads easily to the creation of a suitable
variety of mental objects, whose mode of existence subsequently seems puzzling. Such contemplation is not
what Sartre is exhorting us to when he exhorts us to
reflect; his *réflexion purifiante* is something more difficult
and less satisfying.

The temptation to think of our psychic life as a thing
is of course increased by the fact that this is how other
people think of it. Serious reflexion about one's own
character will often induce a curious sense of emptiness;
and if one knows another person well, one may sometimes intuit a similar void in him. (This is one of the
strange privileges of friendship.) But usually one views
other people as compact finished products to whom

labels ('jealous', 'bad-tempered', 'shrewd', 'vivacious') are attached on the strength of their conduct; and since the myth of 'the ghost in the machine' is so deep in our language we inevitably think of the person as composed of psychic forces which issue in the performances that justify the names. (It is exclusively this aspect of our knowledge of mind which is dealt with in *The Concept of Mind*. The problems of motivation and self-knowledge which Ryle omits and Sartre discusses do not arise if we consider only the sort of knowledge involved in the everyday labelling of our acquaintances.) Our consciousness of how other people label us in this sort of way, and how they see us, is often very acute. This concern is our *être-pour-autrui* of which Sartre has given so many brilliant analyses both in the novels and (more particularly) in *L'Etre et le Néant*. To see ourselves through the eyes of another is to see ourselves suddenly fixed, opaque, complete; and we may well be tempted to accept such a valuation as our own, as a relief from the apparent emptiness of self-examination. On the other hand if we disown that which we apprehend the other as seeing, the experience may be distressing or maddening.

It may now be a little easier to see what sort of a middle way it is that Sartre is trying to take. Traditional metaphysical descriptions of the mind's operations made it seem a strange unobservable entity, separated from our overt doings by a void in which 'psychological experiences' lived uneasily, unable to attach themselves properly to either side. Modern positivism achieves a monistic position by resolving the mind into its outward manifestations. Sartre wishes to do justice to the way in which the mind itself hesitates between monism and dualism—a hesitation which is manifested in real observable modes of experience.

How does Sartre believe that we can defeat our tendency to bad faith? If this were clear the nature of bad faith itself would be clearer. We have already seen that Sartre rejects the idea that ' sincerity ', in the sense of a transparent coincidence with oneself (the ideal of Roquentin and Daniel), is impossible. We have seen too that the realisation of ' value ' seems to depend upon the reflective breaking up of the *empâtement* of consciousness. A value which is identified with a thing, whether material or psychic, is not a value. 'Any value which founded its ideal nature on its being would *ipso facto* cease to be value, and would realise a heteronomy of the will ' (*L'Etre et le Néant*, p. 76). This is the rediscovery of Kant upon which positivist ethics also rests. But while Kant certainly believed (as firmly as Freud) that one should not take one's psychic life at its face value, the rational will which alone was good remained separate from the world of empirical phenomena and unseen in its operation. Kant did not identify value with any empirical act or object—but he did identify it with a particular non-empirical kind of action.

Many aspects of mind can readily be explained in terms of observable *functions* in such a way as to prepare us to let go of the search for the inner *substance*. In a way, character *is* conduct. Or, if a ' deeper ' description is preferred, character *is* the play of unconscious psychic forces. But what about the act of choice itself? This alone seems to bring us back to the egocentric viewpoint which was abandoned when our units of analysis were operations which an outsider could observe. Kant excepted the act of moral choice from the world of phenomena; although in a way he defined it, yet he left its operation mysterious. (I do not *know* the working of the rational will in myself.) Kierkegaard objected to Hegel's dialectical barrel-organ because the egocentric

privacy of the act of choice seemed to be lost in the
objectively determined rational movement of the dialectic.
Sartre, too, cannot accept a reduction of mind to observable phenomena, whether Rylean routines or Freudian
forces. To do this would be to destroy the world's instantaneous kernel, to neglect that which is the sovereign
source of meaning. The consciousness moreover is at
all times sovereign, at all times responsible, since there
is no ' rational nature ' in Sartre's metaphysic to take
over the job of fixing the meaning of even a part of
the universe.

Sartre objects to Freud's analysis of action not only
because Freud seems to make the meaning of the act
something which is in principle determinable by an outside observer independently of the consciousness of the
actor, but also because Freud refers the meaning of the
act to the past. Sartre wishes to refer it to the future;
but in doing so he wishes to avoid an opposition (such
as Kant's picture might suggest) of blind causes to transparent reasons. (As if the act were an unintelligible
leap out of a given empirical situation.) The distinction
to be made in analysing choice is rather that between
the *motif*, or explicit reflective seizure of the world as
pointing towards a certain end, and its correlative, the
mobile, which is my unreflective consciousness of the
situation coloured in a certain way. It is the *mobile*,
the pre-reflective consciousness of how we grasp the
situation, that we often mistake for a causal factor.
Motivation is not a rational causality (Kant) or a psychic
causality (Freud). It has the magical self-enchanting
quality which Sartre has analysed in the *Essay on the
Emotions*. ' The act of will ', the moral reflexion, is
already framed in my unreflective and self-prolonging
conception of how things lie. Liberty lies deeper than
will. It is I who confer value on both the *motifs* and

the *mobiles*; I am not an independent rational observer
who estimates objectively a given situation for which I
am not responsible. Moral reflexion is no more than
the choice of a volitional mode of action rather than
an unreflective mode. *La délibération volontaire est
toujours truquée ... Quand je délibère les jeux sont faits.*[3]

This analysis of choice, negatively considered, seems
not unlike that which is offered by certain positivists.
(See for instance Stuart Hampshire's article in *Mind*
for October 1949. 'The crux is in the labelling.') Such
an account would seem either to run the behaviouristic
risks which Sartre was anxious to avoid (choice is the
de facto pattern of my life) or else, if the psychic background is filled in, to be a more sophisticated kind of
determinism. What of the openness of the future, in
relation to which Sartre wished to give meaning to the
projet of consciousness, what of this liberty which lies
deeper than will? This is to be sought at the level of
the *projet fondamental*, which is the level of a purifying
reflexion, as distinct from the *réflexion complice* which
accompanies the willed deliberation. Elsewhere in a
revealing phrase Sartre says: 'The circularity of: to
speak I must know my thought but how am I to fix my
thought except in words? is the form of all human
reality.' The existent is determined by the not-yet-
existent, and vice versa. Our acts teach us our intention
just as our language teaches us our thoughts; and this
is not the same as to say that our intentions are nothing
but our acts, or our thoughts nothing but our words.
Yet what is the fundamental project, is it a ' free '
project?

It is difficult to give a clear answer, or even a clear
sense, to this question. It is a matter of, as it were,

[3] ' Willed deliberation is always faked. . . When I deliberate
the die is already cast ' (*L'Etre et le Néant*, p. 527).

catching myself at the moment in which I 'give value' to the *motifs* and *mobiles* which seem to determine my choice? To think this would simply be to repeat one stage further back the error of imagining that freedom consists in an immediate act of will. The instantaneous kernel of the world does not exercise a total sovereignty in any moment-to-moment sense. True choice, according to Sartre, consists in the more long term attempt to *assume* our own being by a purifying reflexion. Liberty is not just the 'lighting up' of our own contingency, it is its comprehension and interiorisation. Liberty, like the cure of the neurotic, lies at the level of a total understanding : an understanding which, I think Sartre would agree, we have no guarantee of reaching or foolproof criterion for recognising, although we know well enough in what direction it lies. It seems, after all, to be like Kant's rational will, magnetic and mysterious.

If someone complains that this means that half the time we do not know what we are doing and that it makes the task of living into a perpetual psychoanalysis, then the answer is that this is indeed how Sartre sees the matter. Sartre has complained that traditional philosophy arose from *la réflexion complice*; true philosophy is a systematic kind of purifying reflexion, and its end products are the first principles of 'existential psychoanalysis'. Sartre, like Freud, sees life as an egocentric drama; 'the world is my world' in that it is shaped by my values, projects and possibilities. Sartre wishes however, while attempting to lay bare by a pure reflexion (which corresponds to Husserl's phenomenological reduction) the nature of consciousness, to preserve the sovereignty of the individual psyche as a source of meaning. For him the psyche is coextensive with consciousness. Whereas for Freud the deepest human impulse is sexual, for Sartre it is the urge towards 'self-coincidence' which is the key to our being. Sartre would doubtless not deny that many of his own favourite symbols can be given a sexual meaning (grasped as ways of thinking of the sexual) by this or that person. But he would maintain that the root cause of the fascination of these things is that they symbolise the consciousness itself.[4]

[4] The striking symbol of the petrifying Medusa is interpreted by Freud as a castration fear (*Collected Papers*, vol. v). Sartre of course regards as its basic sense our general fear of being observed (*L'Etre et le Néant*, p. 502). It is interesting to speculate on how one would set about deciding which interpretation was 'correct'.

IX

THE IMPOSSIBILITY OF INCARNATION

There are two kinds of objections to be made to Sartre's theory of consciousness, although it contains, as part of its 'evidence', a vast amount of subtle and revealing psychological analysis. The first objection, taking the whole descriptive project as a possible one, is that it is arbitrary and incomplete. The second objection is methodological, to the effect that Sartre is doing in a different way just what he has accused traditional philosophy of doing, that is, hypostatising the mind in the form of an imaginary and indemonstrable substance.

The speculative arbitrariness of the structure is I think undeniable. Sartre offers nothing like a convincing deduction of his categories. The three modes of consciousness are unreflective awareness, reflexion, and being-for-others. The main world-making categories of consciousness are the forms of our relations with others: language, love, hate, indifference, desire, sadism and masochism. But why should one stop there? According to Sartre the awareness of others is a radical form of our awareness of the world; we do not have to 'infer our friends'. On the other hand, a sense of communal belongingness, a sense of 'we', which is something we often *experience*, is not fundamental to our being, does not make part of the 'ontological structure of the human world' (*L'Etre et le Néant*, p. 485). There is something arbitrary about the idea of a radical or basic category here. Suppose someone maintains that in *his* case the most profound category of the real is his relation to his work—and that he is completely unaware of the attention of his neighbours? Sartre's arguments against such a position could only consist, as do all his arguments in this matter, of very persuasive descriptions, which either ' ring the bell ' or not. The appeal is to our experience, and as a matter of fact the answers are various. What Sartre certainly has given is a brilliant and generally instructive self-analysis. We are tempted to say to him : this is one kind of person, yes : but there are others.

Sartre's work is easily vulnerable to the attack which takes the form of questioning the status of his assertions. Sartre would have done better to admit and to open to investigation the sense in which all *general* descriptions of the mind must belong to *la réflexion complice*; that is, must involve hypostatisations. They are not for that reason misleading or pointless. Only Sartre's theory has point in the way in which all metaphysical theories have point and not in a new way. (All metaphysical theories are inconclusively vulnerable to positivist attack.) What seems new about it is its closeness to theories such as that of Freud which are called ' psychological '. But the same problems of point and status arise about Freud's theories if they are considered in any but a narrowly therapeutic sense. It is more instructive to call Freud's work a sort of metaphysics than to call Sartre's a sort of psychology. The latter remark kills reflexion, the former invites it. It is more profitable to criticise Sartre in the spirit of the first objection, taking it for granted that the line between metaphysics and psychology is not now a clear one.

Sartre praises Kierkegaard for maintaining against Hegel that what I crave from the world is the recognition of my being as an individual, and not as an abstract truth. The essence of Sartre's attempt to describe the mind is the recognition of our contingency in the psychic sphere, combined with the maintenance of the sove-reignty of the individual consciousness. Consciousness is not to be reduced to knowledge or choice to rational causation. That is, Sartre abandons the idealist notion of mind as a self-determining complex of intelligible ideas, while retaining the notion of mind as the source of meaning. It is not a radiant source, however. He pictures it sluggish and dark, implicitly rather than explicitly self-aware, and yet, even in its unreflective times, the responsible creator of sense. No 'meaning' escapes the scope of consciousness, either in the world or in the psyche. The sense of all objects is a human sense, which I responsibly maintain; they are not labelled either by external Nature or by a Rational Self in me. There is no unconscious mind, nothing 'in' the consciousness of which the consciousness is not aware. Only, since we are contingent beings in situations which are 'given' to us, the meanings which we impose are not arbitrary but share that contingency. There is no human 'nature', but there is a human 'situation'.

To say that we are 'responsible' for the categories we use in the natural world seems bizarre, since these categories are so firm an inheritance and shift so slowly; though they do shift, for instance under the influence of science. (Consider how our concept of colour is gradually changing under the impact of popular physics.) 'Responsibility' for this shift moreover, as for the thousand meanings which are not shifting, would seem to be collective rather than individual. Sartre fails to emphasise the power of our inherited collective view of the world—save where it appears in the form of social prejudice and is labelled 'bad faith'. (In effect he regards all unreflective social outlooks as in bad faith.) He is in the unavoidably uncomfortable position of the egocentric philosopher who professes no universal theory of the self. He neglects the sphere of objective publicly determined 'meanings' which scientifically minded

Anglo-Saxon philosophers have too exclusively cultivated. He wishes to think of meaning as the deep rich subjective colours of the world, and yet to stay out of solipsism. It is the unique emotional vision which he wishes to characterise, not that of a scientist in pursuit of universally demonstrable sense. Once again, the dramatic colour of his theory comes from the easily grasped examples of personal conflict.

Yet it is just here that Sartre's solipsistic view of meaning raises difficulties of another kind. He does not fall into the error of which Kierkegaard accuses Hegel, but he does fall into a rather similar one. He isolates the self so that it treats others, not as objects of knowledge certainly, but as objects to be feared, manipulated and imagined about. Sartre's is not a rational but an imaginative solipsism. He comments on the unsatisfactory circularity of our relations with other people. We can never sufficiently respect the liberty of the other: we cannot co-operate wholly in his freedom, or *make* him free, and yet short of that we constitute opaque obstacles in his world. This failure is the root cause of feelings of guilt and sin. Sartre analyses love as a particular case of this frustration. Love is one of the forms under which we pursue stability of being. Stability derives here from the steady adoring gaze of the lover, caught in which the beloved feels full, compact and justified. ' Love is essentially the urge to make oneself loved.' But the lover demands a similar returning gaze, and is free at any moment to withhold his own. If the beloved dominates the lover so as to fix and hold his admiration, this destroys the value of the regard which is only prized so far as it is freely given. If the beloved basks passively before the lover the latter remains unsatisfied. Reciprocal love is therefore precarious, if not impossible, and readily moves towards the satisfactions of sadism or masochism (varieties of domination or basking).

Sartre says of the mental image that it is unsatisfying because it is the slave of consciousness. Unlike the inexhaustible object of perception it is poor and non-resistant, it contains nothing but what I put into it. Sartre presents love, even at its most vigorous, as a dilemma of the imagination. He follows here very closely the account of the enslavement of one consciousness by another which is given by Hegel in the 'Master and Slave' section of the *Phenomenology*. Only Sartre has subjectivised the picture, leaving out the references to work, the 'real' aspect of the enslavement—and incidentally, in Hegel's version, the pointer towards the liberation of the slave. Sartre's lovers are each engaged in perpetual speculation about the attitude of the other. Their project is appropriative, their torment of the imagination. Proust says that what I receive in the presence of the beloved object is a negative which I develop later. This gives the essence of the situation, though Sartre imagines the battle as more directly engaged than this image suggests. There is much psychological acuteness in this account. But as a definition of love it is curiously abstract. If this is what Sartre means by the 'recognition of my being as an individual', then it seems to differ in no essential from that recognition of me as an abstract truth for which he censures Hegel. What each one seems to crave, according to Sartre, is that he should be imaginatively contemplated by the other—a craving which is frustrated because of the reciprocal nature of the demand and because of the loneliness and essential poverty of the imagination. Sartre's lovers are out of the world, their struggle is not an incarnate struggle. There is no suggestion in Sartre's account that love is connected with action and day to

day living; that it is other than a battle between two
hypnotists in a closed room.

For Sartre imagination—which in effect he identifies
with consciousness, it is the 'essential characteristic' of
consciousness—is both liberation and enslavement. It is
the power to set things at a distance. It is also the
tendency towards self-enchantment, the inertia of the
consciousness. This view of imagination is at the root
of Sartre's misunderstanding both of contemplation and
of action. Any imaginative movement which is not the
scattering of a given complex is a piece of self-deception,
a self-protective dodge of the consciousness. Sartre sees
emotion as a dodge of this kind; he does not consider
the problems raised by either 'justified' real emotions
or 'purged' aesthetic emotions. He isolates emotion
from the world; it is an imperious infantile gesture, a
check to freedom, a *comédie*.

This view impoverishes in advance his theory of art.
At the close of *L'Imaginaire*, where he touches on the
matter, Sartre writes : 'aesthetic contemplation is a provoked dream'. This exercise of the imagination too
initially appears as a fall out of freedom, a degradation
and fascination of the consciousness. In the light of the
Essay on the Emotions it is already plain that the artist
must appear, if he is unreflective as a futile escapist
(Roquentin when he was writing the life of the Marquis
de Rollebon), or if he is reflective as engaged upon some
dubious metaphysical project (Roquentin in his final
phase). Emotion as a real creative power, or as part of
a new experience, Sartre does not recognise.

Language is treated by Sartre as a fundamental aspect
of being-for-others. As soon as there is *another*, one who
observes me and interprets the utterances of my behaviour, there is language (*L'Etre et le Néant*, p. 440).
Language is that aspect of me which, in laying me open

to interpretation, gives me away—*le fait même de l'expression est un vol de pensée*[1]—and which may also constitute my defence. In such circumstances the primitive tendency of language will be towards command or seduction. When Sartre comes to elaborate his aesthetic theory in *What is Literature?* he modifies his view, but not fundamentally, and adds a clearer pragmatic corollary. Language (and presumably emotion) may now constitute a structure to be contemplated (poetry); or else both language and emotion will drive us back, after a reflective moment, into the world of tasks (prose). In the latter case any pleasure which the language affords us will be connected with our apprehension of the practical 'engaged' character of the writing.

Sartre has isolated both contemplation and action. Contemplation is the self-enchantment of the imagination. (Contemplative uses of language will *tend* to be lies.) Action is the unreflective world of tasks. In between them there is only the uneasy flickering of the reflective moment. Sartre's lovers are saved neither by their involvement in a communal world of action, nor by a purging of their imagination; their imaginings are conceived as a selfish inertia. (Contrast the *fidélité créatrice* in terms of which a philosopher such as Marcel conceives the loving imagination.) But now, for the sake of his theory of art and politics, Sartre needs to regenerate the imagining spirit and join it to the world of action.

It might seem clear in any case that the only way to regenerate the imagining spirit *is* to join it to the world of action. Love is not futile, not because we live it more imaginatively but because we live it more externally. When Marx said that he wanted not to explain the world but to change it he was not rejecting theory but stating the essence of his own theory. The question is,

[1] 'The very fact of expression is a theft of thought.'

can a Knight of Faith really go on looking like a tax collector?[2] In *L'Etre et le Néant* Sartre seemed to think so. Like Kierkegaard, Sartre is both anti-totalitarian and anti-bourgeois. Sartre's man moves through a society which he finds unreal and alien, but without the consolation of a rational universe. His action seems not to lie *in* this social world; his freedom is a mysterious point which he is never sure of having reached. His virtue lies in understanding his own contingency in order to assume it, not the contingency of the world in order to alter it. It seems as if what ' justifies' him is just this precarious honesty, haunted as it is by a sense of the absolute. Sartre sees our dividedness and yearning sometimes as a flaw and a lack, sometimes as a rather dry mystery, not a rich one like Marcel's, or a vivid one like Berdyaev's. The outside point of view upon the mind, the point of view of history or science, is the point of view of bad faith. The mind must be understood from within, and in a world where objectivity has disappeared with the eye of God, it would seem that each of us can only do this for ourselves. The scene would appear to be set for what George Lukacs in a charming phrase calls the *carnaval permanent de l'intériorité fétichisée* of the western intellectual.[3]

Sartre does suggest in *L'Etre et le Néant* that the way out of the spiritual dilemma which he has depicted is not through art or theology, but by a ' return to existence' which will renew its value. But he does not display this return as any real reintegration of his hero into social life. It savours rather of a ' return' organised from the psychoanalyst's couch, and not pursued into

[2] Kierkegaard's ' Knight of Faith ' bears no visible marks of his nature. He ' looks like a tax-collector ' (*Fear and Trembling*, p. 53).
[3] *Existentialisme ou Marxisme?*, p. 90.

the daily life that lies beyond the case book. Sartre's man is still at the stage of thinking perpetually of himself. He is clear however that his salvation lies in action; and for Sartre action means politics. It is from politics, and not from love, that he learns about the union of the flesh and the spirit. Sartre comes to politics from two points of view. Partly he approaches it as a philosophical solution to a solipsistic dilemma. Partly he meets it as the practical concern of a Western democrat. Sartre has in himself both the intense egocentric conception of personal life and the pragmatic utilitarian view of politics which most western people keep as two separate notions in their head; only since he is a metaphysician Sartre wishes to join the two by a theory of action.

He joins them clumsily, as we have seen. His theory of mind is inspired by a mistrust of the idealist deification of reason and knowledge. *La réflexion purifiante* is not a form of knowledge but a continual *movement* of the spirit which becomes insincere if it is ever still. The reason in which Sartre believes is non-utilitarian and mysterious. What is real in man is this continual upsurge. But on the other hand, Sartre is much too concerned about the historical scene to allow finally that freedom is a matter of conviction or truth a personal *élan*. He has very definite views about political freedom. He needs to reintroduce an objective viewpoint. He does this by a piece of Kantian ethics which enables him to move on into utilitarianism. His view (expressed in *L'Existentialisme est un Humanisme*[4]) that if I will freedom for myself I necessarily will it in the same sense for others goes even beyond Kant. Kant did not specify precisely what the categorical demand or reason would be in any particular case of treating a man as an end.

[4] And set forth much more extensively in the work of Simone de Beauvoir.

Sartre's philosophy already implies a sort of pragmatism; our being is what we do, our world is a world of tasks. It is in connexion with politics alone that he is able to conceive a universal value for this ' doing ', which otherwise remains caught in the privacy of the individual project. It is at this point alone—the point at which the individual is touched by the ideal of liberating mankind from oppression—that Sartre can conceive of a value which will give sense to our activities and bind them together. But he has not provided for this picture the metaphysical background needed to integrate it into his philosophy. He does not believe in a Kantian self which is precisely the same in each of us; the self-stabilising project which he does take to be the essence of the psyche need not (if we follow *L'Etre et le Néant*) become concrete in the form of universal libertarianism. Nor does he have the clear conception of historical causality or of human good needed to make of his theory a utilitarianism similar to that of the Marxist. The action which Sartre advocates to heal the spiritual breach is neither a renewed conception of our daily tasks (such a spiritualisation of work he would deem to be impossible in a bourgeois society) nor is it a confident programme of revolutionary activity. Sartre's world is without a historical perspective, and very deliberately so. The future which seems to him real is the warm living future of the individual project. Reality is not an intelligible object of universal knowledge which can be operated on scientifically so as to bring about a common good. He remains therefore an uneasy utilitarian, hovering on the verge of an irresponsible pragmatism, which has its affinities with the romantic nineteenth-century cult of ' experience '.

Sartre rejects his own society with its inheritance of meanings; he demands a reflective revolt against it. But he knows, as any intellectual knows, that undisciplined reflexion may rot. He has grasped too the idea that thought is to be purged and justified by its integration with a routine of living. But since he rejects not only society but religion, there is no way of living which offers to him the possibility of the yearned for marriage of action and spirit. There is only the uneasy marginal pursuit of the idea of freedom which seems inevitably to fall into corruption as soon as it takes on the form of a political achievement. This uneasy thinking is dominated by the sense, which few intellectuals can think away, of the historical transitoriness of capitalism in its present form. Placed as we are we find it hard to be either convinced dualists or simple empiricists. Sartre's picture of consciousness as a *totalité détotalisé* may be thought of as a sort of myth of our condition. The spirit seems to have deserted our social fabric and to hang in the air, blowing to and fro on the ideological gales. The problem is how to bring it back into our daily life. The Marxists who claim to have achieved a society where doing and believing form a concrete unity have done it at what seems to us too high a cost to the integrity of the individual. A confused sense of the preciousness of this integrity remains to us as an article of faith, and it finds expression too in the philosophy of Sartre.

Sartre described very exactly the situation of a being who, deprived of general truths, is tormented by an absolute aspiration. If this appears to be an exploration of the condition of his contemporaries, it will not be the first time that important philosophical writing will have been of this type. Sartre is enough of a humanist to find this aspiration touching and admirable, enough of a romantic to enjoy adding that it is fruitless, and enough of a politician to introduce a theoretical contradiction for immediate practical ends. His philosophy is not just a piece of irresponsible romanticism; it is the expression of a last ditch attachment to the value of the individual, expressed in philosophical terms. Sartre is performing the traditional task of the philosopher; he is reflecting systematically about the human condition. The role of philosophy might be said to be to extend and deepen the self-awareness of mankind. Such a definition will cover both analysis and metaphysics. What the psychoanalyst does for the particular consciousness of the individual the metaphysician does for the intellectual consciousness of the group he is addressing, and through them perhaps for the consciousness of an epoch. He presents a conceptual framework which is an aid to understanding. The answer to those who wish to eliminate metaphysics is the 'moral' answer : that it is proper for intellectual groups to make this particular sort of effort at self-comprehension. That the influence of such attempts, for good or evil, is not limited to the groups concerned is evident from the history of philosophy.

X

LINGUISTIC ACTS AND LINGUISTIC OBJECTS

I have tried to rest what I have to say about Sartre upon a consideration of his novels. Although Sartre is plainly more at home as a playwright than as a novelist, the novels provide more comprehensive material for a study of his thought; they reveal very clearly both the central structure of his philosophy (*La Nausée*) and the detail of his interest in the contemporary world (*Les Chemins*). I want now in conclusion to discuss Sartre's theory of *la littérature engagée*, and to pass some judgment upon his performance as a novelist.

The novel, the novel proper that is, is about people's treatment of each other, and so it is about human values. A modern critic such as F. R. Leavis concentrates his attention upon this aspect of the novel's subject-matter; he demands that the novelist should be concerned with serious matters and that his total treatment of them should be 'morally mature'. What constitutes ' maturity' is something of which we all have some notion and which could be demonstrated in detail in the case of any particular novel. These considerations will form a large part of our estimate of a novel as a work of literature. But it will clearly not be enough for us to know that the novelist has a mature and interesting viewpoint on human affairs and to know from reading his novel what the viewpoint is; our judgment of him as a novelist will also depend on *how* he incarnates his viewpoint in his literary medium, although to put it thus is misleading if it suggests that the particular viewpoint exists apart from its incarnation.

Sartre could certainly not be accused of a lack of seriousness or of moral maturity. But what about his manner, in the novels, of making his thought concrete? The modern work with which I am most tempted to compare *Les Chemins de la Liberté* is L. H. Myers's trilogy, *The Near and the Far*. This impressive work discusses a large number of philosophical and religious problems through the medium of a group of characters who 'represent' particular ideologies. Yet because we feel that the characters move in order to support the ideas, and that the colour is applied to them in a decorative manner, we are left with the sense that these books are not exactly novels. A certain transmutation of the ideas presented has not taken place. We feel a similar uneasiness in reading *Les Chemins*.

Sartre, be it remembered, approaches literature somewhat in the mood of a physician coming to his patient. Literature, in his view, is sick because of a separation of the writer from life, which has shown itself in either a hatred of language, or an absorption in language for its own sake. The writer has now been forced back to a living contact with the world by being placed in 'extreme situations'. It remains for him to effect the cure of the language by affirming its rôle as a medium of communication. When he discusses this idea in *What is Literature?* Sartre makes a distinction between prose and poetry: with prose we are inside language, with poetry we are outside language. Prose is an extension of our activities, prose words are transparent, prose is simply for communication. Here 'we are within language as within our body' (p.11). This is what he wants to tell the novelist. Whereas for the poet 'language is a structure of the external world' (p. 6). In reading poetry we run up against language in amazement. But prose is an instrument; and 'in prose the aesthetic pleasure is pure only if it is thrown in into the bargain' (p. 15). It is only prose literature, then, which Sartre wishes to see 'committed', and it is only for prose literature that he makes the connexion of 'good writing' with ideological commitment. It is the prose writer who 'has only one subject—freedom'.

There seem to be two theses about the task of prose literature. One is that the language of prose is naturally and properly communicative (as contrasted with the language of poetry), and that the healthy prose writer will not sport with it in a 'poetic' manner, but will use it to make a communication. The other thesis is that since the creation and enjoyment of literature demand a disciplined purging of the mind on the part of the writer and a similar 'free' response from the reader, the literary man has a special interest in the 'free' society; he desires a certain harmony of wills between himself and his readers, and cannot but be concerned about the promotion and preservation of the possibility of a similar free response throughout society at large. The good writer is a natural progressive.

The distinction between prose and poetry seems at first sight an illuminating one. But what exactly does it mean? It seems true that when reading a poem we 'stay at the words'; what the thing *is* is here. As Sartre says of a piece of Rimbaud which he quotes: 'The interrogation has become a thing as the anguish of Tintoretto became a yellow sky. It is no longer a meaning but a substance' (p. 9). The image which suggests itself is that of language as an opaque coagulated substance to be contemplated for itself alone, or else as a transparent glass through which one looks at the world or a tool with which one prods it. Yet in what exactly does the opaque nature of poetry consist? One might guess that the distinction was simply that between discursive and non-discursive, communicative and non-communicative uses of language. Yet this is not in itself a very clear distinction. In an obvious sense many kinds of poetry (e.g. English poetry of the eighteenth century) *are* communicative and discursive, and it would be a sophistry to distinguish the content communicated from the ' poetic ' character of the writing. Much prose, on the other hand, has qualities of form and texture such that it impresses us as a linguistic structure met with from the outside. (Landor, de Quincey, Sir Thomas Browne.) If the distinction is between the rhetorical and densely imaged and the straight-forward, this would seem to cut through the middle of both prose and poetry. There is the transparency of simplicity which is not the same as the transparency of utility. Some poetry consists of opaque mountains of imagery; but at other times we slip, with an ease which is part of the beauty of the thing, straight into the poetic thought. The poetic language of Hopkins is opaque, that of Wordsworth is transparent.

The ' thinginess ' of the poem, that which tempts one to call it a substance, rather than a meaning, does not seem to depend upon the obscurity or complexity of the language or upon whether an intellectual grasp of the ' argument ' forms a part of the enjoying of it. Poetic language may be transparent and discursive, and prose, whether in literary or in everyday use, may be opaque and rhetorical. The tautness, the separateness, the substantial character of the poem cannot be accounted for by any short formula about approaching language from inside or outside. The ' substantiality ' is a function of all the aesthetically relevant properties of the poem, and what these are (imagery, vocabulary, word-order, thought, movement, argument) will vary according to the type of poetry or the particular poem in question. What makes the poem separate is not just the mode of language-using of which it is an instance, but the quality and integrity of the poetic thought of which it is an incarnation. (A bad poem is imperfectly 'substantial'.) But if it is *this* which gives us the sensation of seeing the thing from the outside, may we not say that certain kinds of prose works are similarly seen? The distinction would now seem to be, again, not that between prose and poetry, but between formless non-aesthetic uses of language and disciplined aesthetic uses.

The language which we are completely *inside* is not prose language in general, but certain regions of ordinary practical discourse only. Literary prose language may be transparent in that we brood over the meaning rather than over the sound and order of the words; but it is not language which we are using, and it is not like a tool or an extension of our bodies. It is language which is deliberately disposed so as to conjure up before us some steady and internally coherent thought or image. Ordinary discourse, on the other hand, may be thought of as transparent not only in the sense of not drawing attention to its particular wordy properties, but also in the sense of being useful. It very often does what shouts or gestures or pictures might equally well achieve, when what matters is the achievement. It directs attention to things in the world, it alters courses of action, it arouses feelings and conveys information.

Now Sartre is patently not suggesting that prose literature ought to regard itself as a purely utilitarian practice, to be judged by the value of the actions it inspires. If that were so propaganda sheets, advertisements, religious tracts, and sentimental fantasies could compete on even terms with the great plays and novels. He appeals in general terms to a view of language as tool-like and communicative, an activity among other human activities, to support his contention that prose literature is naturally and properly 'committed'. Yet when he comes to state more precisely what commitment involves he moves on to a second and very different thesis, to the effect that the proper activity of the prose writer is to invite a free and selfless response from his reader and in the process to commend the cause of freedom for all mankind. To achieve this involves a careful, disciplined and reflective use of language which is like neither its everyday tool-like use, where it appears as one activity among others, nor its reflective use as a propaganda weapon. Sartre makes persuasive play with the contrast between the poetic linguistic thing and the prose linguistic act; but the distinction he then makes between the disciplined 'liberating' uses of prose and its other uses disqualifies him from using the force of the first distinction to support his argument.

If the writer ought to be 'progressive' because the work of art is a task set to freedom, then it is hard to see why *any* art should be excluded : the very 'thinginess' of the poem, which Sartre used earlier as an example of the detachment of this art from influence on human affairs, appears to be an example of the achievement of the purged and disciplined appeal which Sartre later takes to be the especial task of the novelist. What can certainly be said is that the novel in particular, since it is a prose work which takes society and human affairs as its theme, is especially suited to making communications and recommendations about social organisation; this is obvious but it is less than what Sartre is maintaining. If moreover it is the disciplined character of aesthetic utterance which inspires a respect for freedom, then not only does there seem no reason to regard the prose writer as more nearly concerned with this liberating activity, but there seems no reason to prefer one sort of artistic subject-matter to another. Here Sartre needs the further equation which connects the ' purging of the emotions ' that is involved in good writing with a respect for human personality which must have progressive political implications.

It may be said that a continuous reflective affirmation is required from the spectator to maintain the structure and separateness of the work of art; it may be illuminating to compare this affirmation with moral evaluation or reiterated acts of faith in an ideological code. But to suggest that therefore there is a *contradiction* involved in lending one's imagination (as author or spectator) to a work which approves of tyranny is to lean too heavily upon the word ' freedom '. It is at such moments that we are most aware of Sartre's hasty rationalism. No *a priori* argument can show that the discipline which produces great art is identical with the discipline of reciprocal human toleration, particularly in the very special sense which Sartre gives to the latter concept.

It might certainly be argued that the great novelist always has some kind of social seriousness. George Lukacs says that the writer is a natural progressive because he is sensitive to the situation of the most suffering class. But this seriousness and sensitiveness then have to be sought and defined in what the writer *shows*, perhaps *malgré lui*, and not in what he professes or sets out to teach.[1] Sartre says that no good novel could be written in praise of anti-Semitism. How does he know? Again it might be argued that such a novel would be somehow self-refuting, that the moral maturity and earnest observation of men which are essential to the writing of a good

[1] See Lukac's chapters on Balzac and Stendhal in *Studies in European Realism*.

novel would here be in contradiction with the doctrine professed. But this is something which would have to be demonstrated in the case of particular novels—in which context terms such as ' moral maturity ' would also find their definition—and not something which can be given sense beforehand in terms of a general theory of human nature.

If we leave theory and look about us all that seems certain is that art may break any rule. That minor art defies Sartre's canons is very clear. It is at least arguable (and if Sartre were right it would be patently false) that Henri de Montherlant, whose political views are reactionary and who despises women, is a better novelist than Sartre who has exemplary opinions on both topics. The discipline which makes de Montherlant a fine writer seems independent of the lamentably unpurged nature of his world outlook. It might however be said that it is the latter which prevents him from being a great writer. Where great art is concerned we are more tempted to insist that there *must* be a connexion between morality and achievement. Hate may take a small writer a long way, but charity must be the quality of a great one. Yet in Shakespeare or in Dostoievsky charity wears a strange and unique face. We are not classifying, but experiencing something new, if we give it that name. Sartre's conception of what the disciplined vision will teach is too confined. He cannot demonstrate that good art will, of its own nature, lead to the treasuring of a particular kind of society. His theory of *la littérature engagée* remains a recommendation to writers concerning their craft, not a demonstration of its essential nature.

His theory gives us however a clue to his own particular virtues and limitations as a novelist. What Sartre requires from art is analysis, the setting of the world in order, the reduction to the intelligible, where the intelli-

gible is something smooth and balanced. *Il faut souffrir
en mesure* is what the little tune says to Roquentin; and
what is *en mesure* is the firm purity which lies at the
opposite pole from the chaos which Roquentin and Sartre
both dread—and also from the darkness which some art
invokes. But Sartre describes the artist's ' evil ' as the
irreducibility of man and the world of thought. Sartre
has an impatience, which is fatal to a novelist proper,
with the *stuff* of human life. He has, on the one hand,
a lively interest, often slightly morbid, in the details of
contemporary living, and on the other a passionate desire
to analyse, to build intellectually pleasing schemes and
patterns. But the feature which might enable these two
talents to fuse into the work of a great novelist is absent,
namely an apprehension of the absurd irreducible uni-
queness of people and of their relations with each other.
Sartre seems blind to the function of prose, not as an
activity or an analytic tool, but as creative of a complete
and unclassifiable image. It is only Sartre's practical
interests that put him in need of speech; his ideal is not
the actual silence of Rimbaud but the intellectual silence
of Mallarmé.

Sartre praises, significantly, what he calls ' the theatre
of situation '. In this type of drama, he says, 'each
character will be nothing but the choice of an issue and
will equal no more than the chosen issue. It is to be
hoped that all literature will become moral and problematic like this new theatre ' (*What is Literature?* p.
217). But an interest in issues rather than people, though
it may sometimes be appropriate for a dramatist, is not
appropriate for a novelist. It is a mark of Sartre's rationalism, his concern after all with essences rather than
existences, that he wishes to model the novel upon the
drama of situation. But though a rationalist *may* be a

good dramatist (Bernard Shaw, whom Sartre resembles in many ways, was both) he is rarely a good novelist. Sartre is certainly a natural playwright (and an excellent one) rather than a novel writer. Many of his scenes (the close of *L'Age de Raison* for instance) could be staged with hardly an alteration; and the carefully constructed clash of towering viewpoints of which *Les Chemins* consists has the harsh emphatic force of drama, rather than the more blurred and detailed working of a novel.

This latter is properly an art of image rather than of analysis; and its revelation is, to borrow Gabriel Marcel's terminology, of a mystery rather than of a problem. But Sartre's special talent is social diagnosis and psycho-analysis; he is at his most brilliant when he dissects some deformed life and lays it out for our inspection, as in *L'Enfance d'un Chef*, where he sketches the growth of a young fascist (in *Le Mur*). The novels are problematic and analytical; and their appeal does in part depend upon our being initially moved by the intellectual conflicts which they resume. All who felt the Spanish War as a personal wound, and all disappointed and vainly passionate lovers of Communism will hear these novels speak to them. But those who, without any pressing concern with these problems, seek their human shape and weight in Sartre's array of people may be left with a sense of emptiness.

Kierkegaard quotes someone as dividing mankind into officers, serving maids and chimney-sweeps—and adds that such a classification ' sets the imagination in motion '. This is the perennial justification of rationalism. Sartre's great inexact equations, like those of his master Hegel, inspire us to reflect. His passion both to possess a big theoretical machine and to gear it on to the details of practical activity compares favourably with the indifference of those who are complacently content to let history get on without them. His inability to write a great novel is a tragic symptom of a situation which afflicts us all. We know that the real lesson to be taught is that the human person is precious and unique; but we seem unable to set it forth except in terms of ideology and abstraction.

BIBLIOGRAPHY

BIBLIOGRAPHY
Works by Sartre (published in Paris unless otherwise stated)

L'Imagination. Librairie Félix Alcan, 1936

La Transcendance de l'ego. Esquisse d'une description phénomenologique. Vrin, 1936–37

La Nausée. Gallimard, 1938

Le Mur. Gallimard, 1939

Esquisse d'une théorie des émotions. Hermann, 1939

L'Imaginaire: Psychologie phénomenonologique de l'imagination. Gallimard, 1940

L'Etre et le néant. Gallimard, 1943

Les Mouches. Gallimard, 1943

Huis clos, in *L'Arbalète*, 1944; Gallimard, 1945

L'Age de raison. Gallimard, 1945. (vol. 1, Les Chemins de la liberté)

Le Sursis. Gallimard, 1945. (vol. 2, Les Chemins de la liberté)

L'Existentialisme est un humanisme. Nagel, 1946

Morts sans sépulture. Lausanne: Marguerat, 1946

La Putain respectueuse. Nagel, 1946

Réflexions sur la question juive. Morihien, 1946. Gallimard, 1954

Baudelaire. Point du Jour, 1946; Gallimard, 1947

Descartes (*Les Classiques de la liberté*). Introduction and selection by J.-P. Sartre. Editions les Trois Collines, 1946

L'Homme et les choses. Seghers, 1947

Situations I. Gallimard, 1947

Les Jeux Sont Faits. Nagel, 1947

Théâtre (*Les Mouches, Huis-Clos, La Putain respectueuse, Morts sans sépultures*). Gallimard, 1947

Les Mains sales, Gallimard, 1948

L'Engrenage. Nagel, 1948

Visages. Seghers, 1948

Situations II. Gallimard, 1948

Orphée noir. (Introduction to *L'Anthologie de la nouvelle poésie nègre et malgache* by Léopold S. Senghor). Presses Universitaires, 1948

La Mort dans l'âme. Gallimard, 1949. (vol. 3, Les Chemins de la liberté)

Situations III. Gallimard, 1949

Entretiens sur la politique (with Gérard Rosenthal and David Rousset). Gallimard, 1949

Le Diable et le bon Dieu. Gallimard, 1951

Saint Genet, comédien et martyr. Gallimard, 1952

L'Affaire Henri Martin. Gallimard, 1953

Kean. Gallimard, 1954

Nekrassov, Gallimard, 1955

Question de méthode (part of Situations II). First published in *Les Temps Modernes*, no. 139, September 1957; Gallimard, 1967, then in *Critique de la raison dialectique*

Les Séquestrés d'Altona. Gallimard, 1959

Critique de la raison dialectique. Gallimard, 1960, Part II, 1986

Marxisme et Existentialisme. Plon, 1962

Les mots. Gallimard, 1963

Situations IV. Gallimard, 1964

Situations V. Gallimard, 1964

Situations VI. Gallimard, 1964

Les Troyennes (an adaptation of Euripides' play). Collection du Théâtre National Populaire, 1965. Gallimard, 1966

Situations VII. Gallimard, 1965

Les Communistes ont peur de la révolution. Didier, 1969

Ecrits de Sartre (a full bibliography of the writings of Sartre up to 1969), Gallimard, 1970. Ed. Michel Contat and Michel Rybalka

Qu'est ce que la littérature? (part of Situations II) Gallimard, 1970

L'Idiot de la famille, vols. 1 and 2, Gallimard, 1971; vol. 3, Gallimard, 1972

Situations VIII. Gallimard, 1972

Situations IX. Gallimard, 1972

Plaidoyer pour les intellectuels. Gallimard, 1972

Un Théâtre de situations. Gallimard, 1973

On a raison de se révolter. Gallimard, 1974

Critiques littéraires 1. Gallimard, 1975

Situations X. Gallimard, 1976

'Sartre par lui-même' (transcript of a filmed interview, directed by Alexandre Astruc and Michel Contat) 1977

Oeuvres romanesques, ed. Michel Contat and Michel Rybalka. Gallimard, 1982

Cahiers pour une morale. Gallimard, 1983

Les Carnets de la drôle de guerre. Gallimard, 1983

Lettres au Castor et à quelques autres, 2 vols. Gallimard, 1983

Le Scénario Freud. Gallimard, 1984

Critique de la raison dialectique. Part II. Gallimard, 1986

Translations into English of works by Sartre

In camera (*Huis clos*) London: Hamish Hamilton, 1946.
New York: *No exit* (in one volume with *The Flies*).
Knopf, 1947

The flies. London: (with *In camera*) Hamish Hamilton,
1946. New York: Knopf, 1947

The age of reason. London: Hamish Hamilton, 1946;
revised trans. Penguin Books, 1961. New York:
Knopf, 1947

Existentialism. New York: Philosophical Library, 1947.
London: *Existentialism and humanism.* Methuen, 1948

The reprieve. New York: Knopf, 1947. London: Hamish
Hamilton, 1948; revised trans. Penguin 1963

The respectful prostitute. London: Hamish Hamilton,
1947. New York: Knopf, 1949.

Portrait of the anti-semite. London: Secker & Warburg,
1948. New York: *Anti-Semite and Jew.* Schocken, 1948

The chips are down. New York: Lear, 1948. London:
Rider, 1951

Psychology of the imagination (*L'Imaginaire*). New York:
Philosophical Library, 1948. London: Rider, 1951

The wall and other stories. New York: New Directions,
1948. London: 'The Wall', included in the short
story collection, *Intimacy.* Hamish Hamilton, 1949

Crime passionel (in *Three Plays*). London: Methuen,
1949. New York: *Dirty hands* (in *Three Plays*) Knopf,
1949

Men without shadows (in *Three Plays*). London: Hamish
Hamilton, 1949. New York: *The Victors* (in *Three
Plays*) Knopf, 1949

The diary of Antoine Roquentin (*La Nausée*). London: John Lehmann, 1949; trans. as *Nausea*. Hamish Hamilton, 1962. New York: *The Diary of Antoine Roquentin*. New Directions, 1949

What is literature? New York: Philosophical Library, 1949. London: Methuen, 1950

Baudelaire. London: Horizon Press, 1949. New York: New Directions, 1950

Iron in the soul. London: Hamish Hamilton, 1950. New York: trans. as *Troubled sleep*. Knopf, 1951

Lucifer and the lord. London: Hamish Hamilton, 1953. New York: *The Devil and the good lord*. Knopf, 1960

In the mesh (*L'Engrenage*). London: Andrew Dakers, 1954

Kean: disorder and genius. London: Hamish Hamilton, 1954. New York: (in one volume with *The Devil and the good lord* and *Nekrassov*) Knopf, 1960

Literary and philosophical essays. London: Rider, 1955. New York: Criterion Books, 1955.

Nekrassov. London: Hamish Hamilton, 1956. New York: (with *The Devil and the good lord*, and *Kean*) Knopf, 1960

Being and nothingness: An essay on phenomenonological ontology. New York: Philosophical Library, 1956. London: Methuen, 1957

Transcendence of the ego. New York: Noonday Press, 1957

Loser wins (*Les Séquestrés d'Altona*). London: Hamish Hamilton, 1960. New York: *The Condemned of Altona*, Knopf, 1961

Outline of a theory of the Emotions. New York: New York Philosophical Library, 1948. London: *Sketch for a theory of the Emotions*. Methuen, 1962

Imagination. Ann Arbor, Michigan: University of Michigan Press, 1962

Search for a method. New York; Knopf, 1963. *The Problem of method*. London: Methuen, 1964

Essays in aesthetics. New York: New York Philosophical Library, 1963. London: Peter Owen, 1964

Saint Genet, actor and martyr. New York: G. Braziller, 1963. London: W. H. Allen, 1964

Words. London: Hamish Hamilton, 1964. New York: trans. as *The words*. Braziller, 1964

Situations (*Situations* IV) London: Hamish Hamilton, 1965. New York: Braziller, 1965

The Trojan women. London: Hamish Hamilton, 1967. New York: Knopf, 1967

The communists and peace (part of *Situations* VI and VII). New York: Braziller, 1968. London: Hamish Hamilton, 1969

The philosophy of Jean-Paul Sartre. London: Methuen, 1968

The spectre of Stalin (part of *Situations* VII). London: Hamish Hamilton, 1969

Politics and literature. London: Calder & Boyars, 1973

Between existentialism and marxism (part of *Situations* VIII and IX). London: New Left Books, 1974. New York: Pantheon Books, 1975

Critique of dialectical reason. Vol 1 *Theory of practical ensembles*. London: New Left Books, 1976. Atlantic Highlands, New Jersey, Humanities Press, 1976

Sartre on theatre. London: Quartet Books, 1976. New York: Pantheon Books, 1976

Sartre in the seventies. (*Situations* X). London: André Deutsch, 1978

The family idiot: Gustave Flaubert, 1821–1857. Chicago and London: University of Chicago Press, vol. 1, 1981

War diaries: notebooks from a phoney war 1939–1940. London: Verso, 1984

The Freud scenario. London: Verso Editions, 1985